SECOND EDITION

Physical Best Activity Guide

Elementary Level

NATIONAL ASSOCIATION FOR SPORT AND PHYSICAL EDUCATION

HUMAN KINETICS

Library of Congress Cataloging-in-Publication Data

Physical Best (Program)
Physical Best activity guide : elementary level / NASPE.
    p. cm.
Includes bibliographical references.
    ISBN 0-7360-4803-0 (soft cover)
        1. Physical education and training--Study and teaching (Elementary)--United States. I. National Association for Sport and Physical Education. II. Title.
GV365.P5 2004

327.86—dc22   2004010137
ISBN: 0-7360-4803-0

Acquisitions Editor: Bonnie Pettifor
Developmental Editor: Jennifer Sekosky
Assistant Editor: Ragen E. Sanner
Copyeditor: Bob Replinger
Proofreader: Kathy Bennett
Permission Manager: Dalene Reeder
Graphic Designer: Robert Reuther
Graphic Artist: Angela K. Snyder, Kathleen Boudreau-Fuoss, Denise Lowry
Photo Manager: Kareema McLendon
Cover Designer: Robert Reuther
Photographer (cover): PhotoDisc Royalty-Free CD
Photographer (interior): Kelly J. Huff, unless otherwise noted
Art Manager: Kelly Hendren
Illustrator (book interior): Kareema McLendon
Illustrator (CD-ROM): Argosy
Printer: United Graphics

We thank Stephen Decatur Middle School in Decatur, Illinois, for assistance in providing the location for the photo shoot for this book, and the faculty of Johns Hill Magnet School and Douglas MacArthur High School, both of Decatur, Illinois, for their assistance in providing the models.

Printed in the United States of America
10 9 8 7 6 5 4 3 2 1

Human Kinetics
Web site: www.HumanKinetics.com

United States: Human Kinetics
P.O. Box 5076
Champaign, IL 61825-5076
800-747-4457
e-mail: humank@hkusa.com

Canada: Human Kinetics
475 Devonshire Road Unit 100
Windsor, ON N8Y 2L5
800-465-7301 (in Canada only)
e-mail: orders@hkcanada.com

Europe: Human Kinetics
107 Bradford Road
Stanningley
Leeds LS28 6AT, United Kingdom
+44 (0) 113 255 5665
e-mail: hk@hkeurope.com

Australia: Human Kinetics
57A Price Avenue
Lower Mitcham, South Australia 5062
08 8277 1555
e-mail: liaw@hkaustralia.com

New Zealand: Human Kinetics
Division of Sports Distributors NZ Ltd.
P.O. Box 300 226 Albany
North Shore City
Auckland
0064 9 448 1207
e-mail: blairc@hknewz.com

CONTENTS

ACTIVITY FINDER

Activity number	Activity title	Activity page	Concept	Primary	Intermediate	Reproducible (on CD-Rom)
3.1	Red Light, Green Light	23	Definition	•		Red, Green, and Yellow Light Cards
3.2	Taking Your Heart Rate	25	Definition		•	Taking Your Heart Rate Station Task Cards
						Taking Your Heart Rate Task Sheet
3.3	Fitness Scavenger Hunt	27	Health benefits		•	Health Benefit Checklist
						Health Benefit Picture Cards
						Color Sequence Cards
3.4	Artery Avengers	30	Health benefits	•		Artery Avenger Assessment Sheet
3.5	Benefit Pickup	32	Health benefits	•		Aerobic Fitness Health Benefit Cards
						Aerobic Fitness Health Benefit Poster
3.6	On Your "Spot," Get Set, Go!	34	Warm-up and cool-down	•		Locomotor Cards
						Warm-Up and Cool-Down Display Cards
3.7	You Should Be Dancing	37	Warm-up and cool-down		•	Dance Step Cards
						Dance Step Descriptions
3.8	Aerobic Activity Picture Chart	39	Frequency	•		Aerobic Activity Picture Chart
3.9	Aerobic Fitness Activity Log	41	Frequency		•	Aerobic Fitness Activity Log
						Activities Goal Contract
3.10	Animal Locomotion	43	Intensity	•		Animal Locomotion Task Cards
3.11	Jumping Frenzy	45	Intensity		•	Jumping Frenzy Instruction Cards
3.12	Pace, Don't Race	47	Time	•		Locomotor, Direction, and Pathway Signs
3.13	Healthy Heart Hoedown	49	Time		•	Dance Cue Cards
3.14	Healthy Heart Tag	51	Type, or specificity	•		Healthy Heart Tag Signs
3.15	You're My Type	53	Type, or specificity		•	You're My Type Instruction Cards
3.16	Aerobic FITT Log	55	Progression		•	Aerobic FITT Log
						Aerobic FITT Log Worksheet
4.1	Mix It Up	63	Definition		•	Mix It Up Station Signs
4.2	Muscle Hustle	67	Definition		•	Muscle Hustle Station Signs
						Muscle Hustle Score Sheet

(continued)

Activity number	Activity title	Activity page	Concept	Primary	Intermediate	Reproducible (on CD-ROM)
5.5	Bend, Stretch, and Move With Ease	112	Warm-up cool-down	•		None
5.6	Mirror and Match	114	Warm-up cool-down		•	None
5.7	Flexibility Activity Picture Chart	116	Frequency	•		Flexibility Activity Picture Chart
5.8	Flexibility Activity Log	118	Frequency		•	Flexibility Activity Log
5.9	At Least 10 Alligators	120	Time	•		At Least 10 Alligators Sign
						At Least 10 Alligators Stretch Cards
						Stretching Reminders
5.10	Roll the Stretch	122	Type, or specificity	•	•	Stretching Picture Charts
						Roll the Stretch Assessment Rubric
						Roll the Stretch Teacher Assessment Rubric
5.11	Sport-Specific Stretch Sentence	124	Type, or specificity		•	Sport-Specific Stretch Worksheet
5.12	Flexibility FITT Log	126	Progression		•	Flexibility FITT Log
						Flexibility FITT Log Worksheet
6.1	Maintaining Balance	132	Definition	•		Body Composition Benefit Signs
6.2	What's the Mix?	134	Definition		•	What's the Mix? Worksheet
6.3	Off the Couch	136	Health benefits	•		Clock Illustration
6.4	Everyday Activities	138	Health benefits		•	Everyday Activities Station Signs
						Everyday Activities Station Recording Chart
6.5	Little Bird Growing Dance	140	Growth and development	•		None
6.6	Nutrition Hunt	142	Nutrition	•		Food Guide Pyramid
6.7	Menu Maker	144	Nutrition		•	Food Guide Pyramid Worksheet
						Menu Maker Worksheet
6.8	Calorie Burn-Up	146	Metabolism	•		None
6.9	Metabolism Medley	149	Metabolism		•	Physical Activity Pyramid for Children

Activity number	Activity title	Activity page	Concept	Primary	Intermediate	Reproducible (on CD-ROM)
7.1	Mind Map Health-Related Fitness Circuit	155	Identifying fitness components; circuit training for *FITNESS-GRAM* assessments, conditioning activities		●	Mind Map Station Signs (each includes definitions, *FITNESSGRAM* assessments, and free choice conditioning activities)
7.2	Fall Into Fitness Circuit	158	Identifying fitness components	●		Fall Into Fitness Circuit Signs
7.3	Harvest Exercise Hunt	160	Circuit training for fitness options		●	Harvest Hunt Task Cards
7.4	Thanksgiving Benefits Circuit	162	Benefits of fitness		●	Thanksgiving Benefits Circuit Station Signs
						Family Homework Assignment— Benefits of Fitness
7.5	The 12 Days of Fitness	165	Fitness components	●	●	12 Days of Fitness Task Cards
						12 Days of Fitness Family Activity Sheet
7.6	Physical Best Crossword Puzzle	168	Concept knowledge assessment		●	Physical Best Crossword Puzzle
7.7	Healthy Heart Exercise Hunt	170	Specificity of training for aerobic fitness (Type)		●	Healthy Heart Exercise Hunt Task Cards
7.8	Heart Smart Orienteering	172	Aerobic fitness and FITT; benefits of activity; warning signs for heart disease and stroke; cooperative learning		●	Orienteering Master Sheet
						Heart Smart Orienteering Questions
						FITT Homework Assignment
7.9	Everyday and Sometimes Foods	175	Nutrition and food choices using the food pyramid		●	Everyday and Sometimes Foods Assessment
						Treat Challenge Sheets
7.10	Spring Into Fitness	178	Total fitness circuit; benefits of activity and risks associated with inactivity		●	Spring Into Fitness Task Cards
7.11	Project ACES	180	Cooperative learning; activity celebration	●	●	Exercise Hunt Task Cards
7.12	Catch the Thrill of the Skill	182	HRF and SRF circuit motor-skill themes integration		●	Health-Related and Skill-Related Fitness Station Signs

(continued)

Activity number	Activity title	Activity page	Concept	Primary	Intermediate	Reproducible (on CD-ROM)
7.13	Dash for Cash	**185**	HR Fitness components, activity celebration	●	●	Dash for Cash Fitness Station Signs
7.14	Summer Fun—Summer Shape-Up Challenges	**188**	Benefits of activity and risks of inactivity	●	●	Summer Shape-Up Challenge Activity Sheet

PREFACE

About Physical Best

Physical Best is a comprehensive health-related fitness education program developed by physical educators for physical educators. Physical Best was designed to educate, challenge, and encourage all children in the knowledge, skills, and attitudes they need for a healthy and fit life. The goal of the program is to help students move from dependence to independence and responsibility for their own health and fitness by promoting regular, enjoyable physical activity. The purpose of Physical Best is to educate *all* children, regardless of athletic talent, physical and mental abilities or disabilities. Physical Best implements this goal through quality resources and professional development workshops for physical educators.

Physical Best is a program of the National Association for Sport and Physical Education (NASPE). A nonprofit membership organization of over 18,000 professionals in the sport and physical education fields, NASPE is an association of the American Alliance for Health, Physical Education, Recreation and Dance dedicated to strengthening basic knowledge about healthy lifestyles among professionals and the general public. Putting that knowledge into action in schools and communities across the nation is critical to improved academic performance, social reform, and the health of individuals.

Overview of Physical Best Resources

This guide contains the information you need to help kindergarten through fifth grade students gain the knowledge, skills, appreciation, and confidence to lead physically active, healthy lives. The easy-to-use instructional activities have been developed and used successfully by physical educators across the United States. You will find competitive and noncompetitive activities, demanding and less demanding activities, and activities that allow for maximum time on task. Above all, the activities are designed to be educational and fun! Packaged with the book is a CD-ROM containing reproducible charts, posters, and handouts that accompany the activities. New features for the second edition include many new activities in each chapter, a sample newsletter for each component of fitness, as well as the addition of a new chapter, titled "Special Events," containing activities that coincide with national holidays and health observances throughout the school year.

This book has two companion resources:

■ *Physical Education for Lifelong Fitness: The Physical Best Teacher's Guide, Second Edition* is a comprehensive guide to incorporating health-related fitness and lifetime physical activity into physical education programs. The guide provides a conceptual framework based on recent research, covering topics such as behavior, motivation and goal setting, health-related fitness curriculum development and teaching methods, components and principles of fitness, and inclusion in health-related fitness and health-related fitness assessment. The guide also contains a wealth of practical information and examples from experienced physical educators. The second edition has streamlined and reorganized many of the chapters, added practical information, a glossary, and resources for physical educators, and updated information and references throughout the text.

■ *Physical Best Activity Guide: Middle and High School Levels, Second Edition* is similar in scope to the elementary guide but is geared toward 6th- through 12th-grade students. The information is more in-depth and allows for a deeper and richer understanding of the importance of daily physical activity. The middle school and high school level guide contains an additional section focused on personal health and fitness planning. This provides students with an introduction to the skills needed to be physically active for life after they graduate from high school. Other features for the second edition include the addition of a CD-ROM containing printable materials that supplement the activities, many new activities in each chapter, and the addition of a new activity chapter, titled "Combined Component," that incorporates multiple health-related fitness components.

Related Resources

During a typical school year, many educators will use more than one program and a variety of teaching resources, overlapping different approaches on a day-to-day basis. With this in mind, it may be reassuring to know that although Physical Best is designed to be used independently for teaching health-related fitness, the following resources can also be used in conjunction with the Physical Best program. *FITNESSGRAM/ACTIVITYGRAM, Fitness for Life* and the NASPE products listed in this section are suggested resources to complement Physical Best.

FITNESSGRAM/ACTIVITYGRAM

FITNESSGRAM/ACTIVITYGRAM (developed by the Cooper Institute) is a comprehensive health-related fitness and activity assessment as well as a computerized reporting system. All elements within *FITNESSGRAM/ACTIVITYGRAM* are designed to assist teachers in accomplishing the primary objective of youth fitness programs, which is to help students establish physical activity as a part of their daily lives.

FITNESSGRAM/ACTIVITYGRAM is based on a belief that extremely high levels of physical fitness, while admirable, are not necessary to accomplish objectives associated with good health and improved function. It is important for all children to have adequate levels of activity and fitness. *FITNESSGRAM/ACTIVITYGRAM* is designed to help all children and youth achieve a level of activity and fitness associated with good health, growth, and function.

FITNESSGRAM/ACTIVITYGRAM resources are published and available through Human Kinetics, as are the materials for the Brockport Physical Fitness Test, which is a health-related fitness assessment for students with disabilities.

Fitness for Life

Fitness for Life is a complete set of resources for teaching a lifetime fitness and wellness course at the secondary level. It is compatible with the Physical Best program in philosophy, with the goal of lifelong physical activity habits, and *Fitness for Life* is a program that has been shown by research to be effective in promoting physically active behavior after students finish school.

Fitness for Life and Physical Best complement one another effectively, because the *Physical Best Activity Guide: Middle and High School Levels, Second Edition* can be used both before and after a *Fitness for Life* course, as well as during the course to provide supplemental activities. Both programs are based on the HELP philosophy, which promotes health for everyone with a focus on lifetime activity of a personal nature. In fact, the two programs are so compatible that the Physical Best program offers teacher training for *Fitness for Life* course instructors.

NASPE Resources

NASPE publishes many additional useful and related resources that are available by calling 800-321-0789 or through the online AAHPERD store at www.aahperd.org:

- *Moving Into the Future: National Standards for Physical Education*
- *Beyond Activities: Learning Experiences to Support the National Physical Education Standards*
- *Appropriate Practices Documents (elementary, middle school and high school)*
- Assessment Series—titles relating to fitness and heart rate
- *Physical Activity for Children: A Statement of Guidelines for Children Ages 5-12*

Physical Best Certification

Physical Best provides accurate, up-to-date information and training to help today's physical educators create a conceptual and integrated format for health-related fitness education within their programs. NASPE/AAHPERD offers a certification program that allows physical education teachers to become Physical Best Health-Fitness Specialists. The Physical Best certification has been created specifically for the purpose of updating physical educators on the most effective strategies for helping their students gain the knowledge, skills, appreciation, and confidence needed to lead physically active, healthy lives. It focuses on application—how to teach fitness concepts through developmentally and age-appropriate activities.

To earn certification through NASPE/AAHPERD as a Physical Best Health-Fitness Specialist, you will need to do the following:

- Attend the one-day Physical Best Health Fitness Specialist Workshop.
- Read this book, *Physical Education for Lifelong Fitness: The Physical Best Teacher's Guide, Second Edition*, and the *FITNESSGRAM/ACTIVITYGRAM Test Administration Manual*.
- Using the required resources mentioned above, complete a take-home examination and submit it to NASPE/AAHPERD. Successful and timely completion and submission to NASPE/AAHPERD will result in certification.

For more information or to learn about becoming a Physical Best Health-Fitness Specialist or Instructor (to train other teachers), call Physical Best at 800-213-7193.

ACKNOWLEDGMENTS

Many educators contributed their time and expertise to this project, beginning with reviews of the first edition by many of the Physical Best Steering Committee members and Physical Best Instructors from around the country. We would like to thank Margie Miller (Missouri), who wrote the report for this book, synthesizing feedback from multiple sources and detailing a comprehensive list of recommendations for the second edition.

In addition to the overall guidance of the Physical Best Steering Committee, the following individuals contributed new activities or significant editorial input for this edition:

Ellen Abbadessa
Arizona

Brenda Belote
Virginia

Michael Bishoff
Maryland

Bill Brady
Virginia

Renee Butler
Missouri

Denise Chenoweth
Maryland

Susan Forman
Arizona

Jennie Gilbert
Illinois

Krista Gillette
New York

Linda Hatchett
Alabama

Colleen Porter Hearn
Virginia

Jill Humann
New Jersey

Melody Kyzer
North Carolina

Lauren Lieberman
New York

Michael Mason
Maryland

Carolyn Masterson
New Jersey

Joan Morrison
Maryland

Sally Nazelrod
Maryland

Carolyn Nelson
Ohio

Angie Odom
Missouri

Janice O'Donnell
New Hampshire

John Perna Jr.
Maryland

Anthony Santillan
Arizona

Kim Sinkhorn
Ohio

Diane Tunnell
Washington

Lisa Weiland-Foster
Hawaii

Jeanine Wert
New York

Debbie Wilkinson
Arizona

An extra note of thanks goes to Ellen Abbadessa, who served as primary contributor and editor for the new "Special Events" chapter; to Jennie Gilbert, Jill Humann, and Carolyn Masterson who greatly assisted in the review and editing stage; and to Brenda Belote, Bill Brady, and Lauren Lieberman; and her students, Jeanine Wert and Krista Gillette, for editing and contributing to the new "Inclusion Tips" portion of each activity. Thanks also to Gayle Claman, program administrator for Physical Best, who played a significant role in coordinating the revision.

Sponsorship

NASPE would like to thank Mars, Inc. and FlagHouse/Cateye Fitness (official equipment sponsor) for their financial and developmental support of the Physical Best program.

The Physical Best program has been reviewed by the American Heart Association and is consistent with their science and recommendations for physical activity.

© 2004 American Heart Association, Inc.

® Mars is a registered trademark of Mars, Incorporated and its affiliates. It is used with permission. Mars, Incorporated is not associated with the National Association for Sport and Physical Education, Human Kinetics, or Dalene Reeder, © Mars, Incorporated 2004.

Reprinted, by permission, from Flaghouse® , 2004.

© 2004 Cateye Fitness, Osaka, Japan.

PART I

Introduction

Teaching Elementary Level Health-Related Fitness

Chapter Contents

- National Standards for Physical Education

- National Health Education Standards

- National Standards for Dance Education

- Integrating Physical Best Into the Elementary Physical Education Curriculum

  Physical Best Activity Template

- Summary

© Human Kinetics

For foundation in teaching health-related fitness activities, we look first to national standards. Many of the national standards that have been developed for physical education, health, and dance can be applied to teaching health-related fitness activities. In the first part of this chapter, we list the national standards from these areas and emphasize the standards that are addressed most often when teaching health-related fitness.

The chapter ends with a brief summary of how Physical Best can be incorporated in a physical education curriculum at the middle and high school levels and a detailed look at the Physical Best activity template. All of the activities in this book follow this template, and the explanations provided in this chapter will help you choose the right activity for the right group of students. You can also use this template as a guide for developing your own activities.

National Standards for Physical Education

The national standards for physical education are based on the definition of the physically educated person as defined by the NASPE Outcomes of Quality Physical Education Programs (NASPE 1992). According to this document, a physically educated person

- has learned skills necessary to perform a variety of physical activities;
- is physically fit;
- participates regularly in physical activity;

National Standards for Physical Education

Physical activity is critical to the development and maintenance of good health. The goal of physical education is to develop physically educated individuals who have the knowledge, skills, and confidence to enjoy a lifetime of healthful physical activity. A physically educated person:

Standard 1
Demonstrates competency in motor skills and movement patterns needed to perform a variety of physical activities

Standard 2
Demonstrates understanding of movement concepts, principles, strategies, and tactics as they apply to the learning and performance of physical activities

Standard 3
Participates regularly in physical activity

Standard 4
Achieves and maintains a health-enhancing level of physical fitness

Standard 5
Exhibits responsible personal and social behavior that respects self and others in physical activity settings

Standard 6
Values physical activity for health, enjoyment, challenge, self-expression, and/or social interaction

■ knows the implications of and the benefits from involvement in physical activities; and

■ values physical activity and its contributions to a healthful lifestyle.

NASPE intended for all five parts of the definition "not to be separated from each other" (NASPE 1992). The definition was further delineated into 20 outcome statements. The definition and outcome statements were used as the basis for the development of the National Standards for Physical Education, originally published by NASPE in 1995 and revised in 2004. The standards define what a student should know and be able to do as a result of a quality physical education program.

Although all standards are taught to some extent through and during health-related fitness education, two standards are emphasized:

Standard 3: Participates regularly in physical activity

Standard 4: Achieves and maintains a health-enhancing level of physical fitness

National Health Education Standards

The National Health Education Standards published in *Achieving Health Literacy* (Joint Committee on National Health Education Standards 1995) are linked to the physical education standards. Health education affords unique knowledge about maintaining health, preventing disease, and reducing risk factors in all situations and settings—and it helps to influence behaviors that promote these aims. These goals relate not only to physical activity but also to other areas of personal, family, and community life.

National Health Education Standards

Standard 1
Students will comprehend concepts related to health promotion and disease prevention.

Standard 2
Students will demonstrate the ability to access valid health information and health-promoting products and services.

Standard 3
Students will demonstrate the ability to practice health-enhancing behaviors and reduce health risks.

Standard 4
Students will analyze the influence of culture, media, technology, and other factors on health.

Standard 5
Students will demonstrate the ability to use interpersonal communication skills to enhance health.

Standard 6
Students will demonstrate the ability to use goal-setting and decision-making skills to enhance health.

Standard 7
Students will demonstrate the ability to advocate for personal, family, and community health.

Health standards 1, 3, and 6 are most closely related to fitness education.

Standard 1: Students will comprehend concepts related to health promotion and disease prevention.

Standard 3: Students will demonstrate the ability to practice health-enhancing behaviors and reduce health risks.

Standard 6: Students will demonstrate the ability to use goal-setting and decision-making skills to enhance health.

National Standards for Dance Education

The National Standards for Dance Education (NDA 1996) are also linked to physical education. Dance is both a movement form (as are sports, aquatics, fitness activities, and outdoor recreational activities) and a physical activity that provides health and fitness benefits. As a physical activity, however, dance is unique in that it is also an art form, affording opportunities to create, communicate meaning, and interpret cultural issues and historical periods.

For the purposes of these materials, standard 6 is of primary importance in health-related fitness education.

Standard 6: Making connections between dance and healthful living

Integrating the national standards in physical education, health, and dance provides an important way to promote the effects of physical activity on health and one's personal

National Standards for Dance Education

What every young American should know and be able to do in dance:

Standard 1
Identifying and demonstrating movement elements and skills in performing dance

Standard 2
Understanding choreographic principles, processes, and structures

Standard 3
Understanding dance as a way to create and communicate meaning

Standard 4
Applying and demonstrating critical and creative thinking skills in dance

Standard 5
Demonstrating and understanding dance in various cultures and historical periods

Standard 6
Making connections between dance and healthful living

Standard 7
Making connections between dance and other disciplines

National Dance Standards 1-7 (pp. 6-9)—These quotes are reprinted from the *National Standards for Arts Education* with permission of the National Dance Association (NDA) an association of the American Alliance for Health, Physical Education, Recreation and Dance. The source of the National Dance Standards (*National Standards for Dance Education: What Every Young American Should Know and Be Able to Do in Dance*) may be purchased from: National Dance, 1900 Association Drive, Reston, VA 20191-1599; or telephone (703) 476-3421.

choice to be physically active. None of these disciplines stands alone. Few student groups are focused on just one purpose, whether in health, competition, or aesthetics. Although some students have a greater interest in or more facile learning style for one of these areas, all youngsters benefit from learning and applying these standards. The recognition of these interdisciplinary links helps us maximize our energies for teaching and learning essential content of all three disciplines.

Integrating Physical Best Into the Elementary Physical Education Curriculum

The *Physical Best Activity Guide: Elementary Level, Second Edition* is more than a compilation of elementary activities that children participate in during their physical education classes. The guide provides instruction for physical education teachers to help children learn about physical fitness and understand the importance of being healthy and leading physically active lives. Physical fitness concepts are taught through the described activities in the book. Therefore, the *Physical Best Activity Guide: Elementary Level, Second Edition* is an integral part of an elementary health and physical education curriculum.

Physical Best activities vary in length of time to complete and may further vary based on class size, classroom environment, and so forth. Because the activities vary in length, a combination of activities can serve as an entire lesson or individual activities can be infused into other lesson plans. The activities provide ideas and resources for teachers to use during their health and physical education lessons, for homework assignments, and through extracurricular activities and special events. Reproducibles found on the CD-ROM provide visual aids and extensions of the activities to help children better understand the concepts taught within the activities.

Physical Best activities instruct children about the principles of training and the importance of being physically active and fit. The activities teach children the concepts of warm-ups and cool-downs, frequency, intensity, time, type, progression, and overload. Furthermore, the activities are fun and challenging. Physical Best emphasizes individuality, encourages students to participate to the best of their ability, and accentuates the importance of participation in regular physical activity on all or most days of the week. Competition is kept to a minimum and is often introduced only as part of the child's inherent motivation to do his or her best when participating in playful activity.

Through Physical Best, teachers are able to instruct children about health-related fitness while also teaching about movement principles and motor skills. Therefore, children learn to travel using different locomotor patterns, moving their bodies in different levels and pathways. They learn that movement increases their heart rates and makes their muscles stronger. Children practice manipulative skills such as throwing, catching, and kicking and at the same time learn several sport-related stretches and muscular endurance activities. Integrating the concepts and sport skills enables children to discover the benefits of being strong and flexible.

Finally, teachers who regularly work with children can instruct them to self-assess health-related fitness levels. Practicing the *FITNESSGRAM* assessments and the Physical Best activities throughout the year enables adolescents to learn about their physical fitness levels and what it takes to become healthier. Moreover, the Physical Best program instructs teachers to involve children in physical activity outside school. Physical Best endorses the Presidential Active Lifestyle Award (PALA) given by the President's Council on Physical Fitness and Sports to recognize the importance of performing fun fitness activities in and outside school. Children learn to record how much physical activity they perform on their own or with their friends, family members, and others in the local community. More information on teaching strategies for health-related fitness can be found in *Physical Education for Lifelong Fitness: The Physical Best Teacher's Guide, Second Edition.* Information on the PALA can be found at: www.presidentschallenge.org.

Physical Best Activity Template

Activities that help students learn while doing are the most successful for teaching lifelong fitness. The *Physical Best Activity Guides* provide a wealth of activities designed specifically to help students learn through doing.

These activities provide a great start to developing an excellent program, but you'll want to add more activities especially suited for your students. Following is a step-by-step explanation of the Physical Best activity template that can also serve as a guide for developing your own activities.

LEVEL

Carefully consider the level of the students for whom you are developing the activity. You can easily modify many activities up or down for students of varying ages and abilities.

CONCEPT

The activity teaches one or more concepts, written in language appropriate to the level of the students. Physical Best includes activities for defining the component of fitness and teaching the health benefits for that component, for warm-up and cool-downs, the FITT Guidelines, and progression and overload. (The chapters "Body Composition" and "Special Events" follow a different format but still list the concept or concepts taught.)

PURPOSE

This component of the template states the student-centered objectives, describing what you want the students to learn.

RELATIONSHIP TO NATIONAL STANDARDS

This component explains which of the national standards in physical education, health education, and dance education the activity addresses.

EQUIPMENT NEEDED

This component lists everything needed to conduct the activity.

REPRODUCIBLE

This component lists what can be found on the accompanying CD-ROM to support the activity. These include charts, signs, task cards, student worksheets, and so forth. You are encouraged to print the reproducibles that appear on the CD-ROM. They are created for letter-sized paper, but can be enlarged according to your needs. Each is labeled by activity number and reproducible title to help you keep them organized.

PROCEDURE

This component lists steps to conduct the activity, including an introduction (called set-induction in the first edition), activity steps and directions, and closure.

TEACHING HINTS

This component of the template offers ideas for variations, extensions, and increases or decreases in level (for example, notes about intensity, ability groupings, and challenges), as well as safety tips and other ideas for effectively teaching the activity.

SAMPLE INCLUSION TIP

This component offers one or more tips for adapting the activity to meet the needs of students with varying abilities and health concerns. Note that a tip for one activity may be useful for other activities as well.

ASSESSMENT

This component explains how you or the students will know that they have learned the information stated in the purpose. Assessment may include teacher discussion, student feedback and review, homework assignments, and so on.

Summary

When you use Physical Best, you are teaching the applicable standards through activity in an age-appropriate and sequential manner. Using the activity template will ensure that your activities are educational and easy to administer. Choose activities that fit into your lesson plans, and you will teach and reinforce important fitness concepts throughout the year. Most importantly these activities have been developed by physical educators for physical educators and have been "real world tested" to ensure that they not only teach the concepts, but also allow students to have fun while performing physical activity.

CHAPTER

2

Introduction to Health-Related Fitness Concepts

Chapter Contents

© Human Kinetics

This chapter provides an introduction to the principles of health-related fitness education. An introduction to the components of health-related fitness can be found at the beginning of each corresponding chapter in Part II, and can be used as a quick reference when teaching the activities in that chapter. For more in-depth study and explanation of these concepts, please refer to *Physical Education for Lifelong Fitness: The Physical Best Teacher's Guide, Second Edition* (2005), as there are several new concepts that are different from the previous edition, especially in the aerobic fitness chapter.

Health-Related Fitness

In teaching health-related fitness, we should not lose sight of the importance of physical activity and the development of fun activities that encourage children to be active. Physical Best has consistently emphasized the development of physical fitness as a lifelong process of active lifestyles, rather than the product of actually being physically fit or the outcome of exercise performed on a regular basis. The focus of our lessons should not be on developing physically fit children, but to teach children basic concepts, skills and the value of physical activity so that they will be competent to participate in activities now and in the future.

Research points to three main reasons children participate in leisure-time activity and sports (Weiss 2000):

- The development and demonstration of physical competence (athletic skills, fitness, physical appearance)
- Social acceptance and support from friends, peers, and significant adults
- Participation in fun activities promoting positive experiences

As you use the Physical Best materials, keep the following definitions in mind to assist you in motivating your students to become physically active, thereby initiating the long path to lifetime fitness and associated health benefits. *Physical fitness* is defined as a set of attributes that people have or achieve relating to their ability to perform physical activity, while *physical activity* is defined as any bodily movement produced by muscle contraction and increases energy expenditure (USDHHS 1996; NASPE 2004b). Since motivation to be physically active does not come from knowing and appreciating the health benefits of increased activity, it is important to impress upon children that being physically active enables them to play longer without getting tired and older students will have more energy for leisure activities; all of which yield health benefits unbeknownst to the child.

Principles of Training

The *overload principle* states that a body system must perform at a level beyond normal in order to adapt and improve physiological function and fitness. You can increase the overload by manipulating the frequency, intensity or duration (time) of an activity. To best explain overload to children, let them experience it firsthand—keep track of the number of minutes they can sustain an activity or how many repetitions they can perform. You may also use a backpack with books or weights and monitor heart rate without the backpack and then with the backpack, explaining how the body will adapt to the heavy load, and later be able to do the same load with less effort.

Progression refers to *how* an individual should increase the overload. It is a gradual increase in the level of exercise and also may be manipulated by increasing the frequency, intensity, time or a combination of all three components. Children should understand that improving their level of fitness is an ongoing process.

Emphasize that all progression must be gradual to be safe. If the overload is applied too soon, the body does not have time to adapt and the benefits may be delayed or an injury may occur; both of which can discourage or prevent an individual from participating. For example, a young child may progress from performing a reverse curl-up, whereby they focus on lowering the body, and work toward performing a regular curl-up. You may also use this same strategy with push-ups, first focusing on the lowering phase, and as the child progresses they will gain strength to perform the complete push-up. The objective is to challenge students, but also create opportunity for success.

To help them better understand progression and see that they are improving, give them opportunities to track their progress (keep a journal). You can also effectively help them achieve this understanding through the use of pretests and posttests.

Specificity states that explicit activities targeting a particular body system must be performed to bring about fitness changes in that area. For example, you must perform aerobic activities that stress the cardiorespiratory system if you want to improve aerobic fitness. This principle applies to all areas of health-related and skill-related fitness; and can also apply within a single area of fitness. For example, performing a biceps curl will increase the strength of the bicep muscle, but has no effect on the leg muscles.

The premise behind the *regularity principle* is based on the old adage of "use it, or lose it." Any fitness gains attained through physical activity are lost if we do not continue to be active. Recognize that the body needs a limited amount of recovery time between bouts of exercise. Too little recovery time may lead to injury or overtraining, and too much time between activity sessions can lead to detraining, or loss of the acquired benefits of physical activity and fitness. The time of recovery also varies by the area of health-related fitness. For example, ACSM recommends three alternate days per week for strength and endurance activities, while daily activity is best for improving one's flexibility; likewise, the minimum frequency for aerobic improvement is three days per week, while five to seven days is optimal. Try to emphasize consistency in activity and not training and conditioning unless you are coaching athletes. Alternatively, remember that recommendations for children's physical activity include daily activity versus the traditional ACSM adult model.

The *individuality principle* takes into account that each person begins at a different level of fitness, has personal goals and objectives for physical activity and fitness, and different genetic potential for change. Although changes in children's physiological responses to training and conditioning are often difficult to measure due to confounding problems with changes associated with the normal growth and maturation process, recognize that students in your classes will respond differently to the activities you prepare for class. Some will improve, some will not; some will enjoy the activities, while others will not; and your job is to provide plenty of opportunities for choice in your classroom, taking into account each student's initial fitness level and personal goals.

FITT Guidelines

Physical Best activities apply the FITT Guidelines to improve health and fitness. The acronym FITT describes the Frequency (how often), the Intensity (how hard), the Time (how long), and the Type (what kind) of activity necessary for improving and maintaining fitness. It also provides the "recipe" for safely applying the previously described principles of training. As you apply these guidelines to children, remember they are not miniature adults, and the adult exercise prescription model should not be applied until the child is at the secondary level. Refer to the Teacher's Guide for detailed explanations of the FITT Guidelines and new recommendations concerning the use of these guidelines with children.

The Activity Session

Whether you are teaching kindergarteners or high school seniors, share the purpose of the lesson and how the day's activity will help them reach a class goal(s) or personalized goal(s). Every activity should incorporate a systematic approach to ensure not only safety but also to prepare the body for the rigors of the workout. The main physical activity must also be developmentally appropriate for students to feel and understand, through participation, the importance of being physically active. Cool-down time should also be incorporated and can be used as time to review and assess learning.

Summary

For the prepubescent child, the emphasis should be placed on increasing physical activity, skill development, and access to a wide variety of sports and activities that may serve as a primer or foundation for conditioning programs during puberty and beyond. Keep in mind that fitness is a journey, not a destination; and the goal is to progress toward self-assessment and self-delivery of health-related fitness activities. Are you and your students ready for the fun of leading a physically active life? If so, progress to the activities that follow.

PART II

Activities

CHAPTER

3

Aerobic Fitness

Chapter Contents

- Defining Aerobic Fitness
- Teaching Guidelines for Aerobic Fitness
- Training Methods for Aerobic Fitness
- Motor Skill Development Through Aerobic Fitness
- Aerobic Fitness Newsletter
- Activities

© Human Kinetics

As we examine the concept of aerobic fitness in children, we should recognize that research in this area is limited. We should not rely on aerobic fitness testing to indicate endurance performance in children, nor should we develop aerobic training programs that parallel the adult exercise prescription model. Although the relationship between physical activity and aerobic fitness is weak in children (Rowland 1996, p. 112), our goal is to enhance the quality and productivity of every child's life through physical education. Refer to *Physical Education for Lifelong Fitness: The Physical Best Teacher's Guide, Second Edition* (2005) and *Developmental Exercise Physiology* (Rowland 1996) for more information concerning the relationship of physical activity and aerobic fitness in children.

Defining Aerobic Fitness

Aerobic fitness is the "ability to perform large muscle, dynamic, moderate to high intensity exercise for prolonged periods" (ACSM 2000, p. 68). To a child this definition may mean the ability to play longer without becoming tired. Many field tests are available to assess aerobic fitness. Physical Best endorses *FITNESSGRAM/ACTIVITYGRAM* (The Cooper Institute 2004). The Brockport Test (Winnick and Short 1999) may be used with students with disabilities.

Many health benefits are associated with physical activity (USDHHS 1996; Blair et al. 1995; Boreham et al. 1997; and Boreham et al. 2001). A recent report by the California Department of Education (2002) indicated that higher levels of fitness in children were associated with higher academic performance on standardized testing. This supports the concept that increased physical activity may help to increase a student's capacity for learning (USDHHS 1996). Remember that children are concrete learners and that the benefits of health-related fitness may not mean much to them at this level. To enhance understanding, you must connect the benefits to something that they can relate to and experience personally and immediately (I can win the race on the playground.). Potential health benefits include the following:

- Strengthens the heart (lower resting and working heart rate, faster recovery)
- Decreases blood pressure
- Strengthens muscles and bones
- Increases energy (to play longer)
- Allows performance of more work with less effort (carry my toys without becoming tired or needing help)
- Reduces stress and tension (get along better with others)
- Enhances appearance and feeling of well-being; improves quality of life
- Improves ability to learn (get homework done faster)
- Promotes healthy body composition
- Increases self-confidence and self-esteem (greater social opportunities)
- Enhances sleep
- Improves lipid profile (increases HDL [good cholesterol], decreases triglycerides)
- Weight control

Our health and well-being change constantly throughout our lives, including the years during childhood. But most children have little interest in the health benefits that they may later recognize in adulthood. At the elementary level, you should select activities that develop and encourage active lifestyles, ultimately leading to improved quality of life. Introduce health-related benefits in a language that children understand, and repeat those benefits in activities across the curriculum. Develop detail and emphasize optimal adult health benefits as children progress through school.

Teaching Guidelines for Aerobic Fitness

Teach fitness concepts through physical activity, minimizing classroom lessons in which students are inactive. Primary grade students should focus on locomotor skills—moving in personal space, exploring fast and slow movement and high and low movement, and learning to work together, including reacting to each other. Circuits or station activities provide excellent opportunity to challenge students independently, develop motor skills, and develop health-related fitness. Keep your groups small, no larger than five at a station. Activities for grades 3 through 5 should include manipulating objects in and through space, gradually including speed and accuracy, and incorporating cooperative learning activities.

In selecting and performing activities, follow the training principles outlined in chapter 5 of *Physical Education for Lifelong Fitness: The Physical Best Teacher's Guide, Second Edition* to develop aerobic fitness. This section contains new material, and you will notice that planning a lesson around attaining a specified target heart rate is not appropriate for elementary or middle school children. Children in primary grades can monitor intensity levels by monitoring their breathing rate and body heat or by placing a hand over the heart and using terms like *slow* (turtle) or *fast* (race car) to describe heart rate. Intermediate-level students (grades 3-5) can begin to locate the carotid and radial arteries, but do not use target heart rate zones at this level. You should not expect most students in elementary school to calculate target heart rate values. This task is more appropriate for middle and high school students. In any case, avoid the use of target heart rate zones as requirements for participation in physical activity. Table 3.1 provides information on how to apply the FITT Guidelines for elementary (5- to 12-year-old) youth.

Remember that alternating cycles of vigorous activity followed by a recovery period characterize the level and tempo of children's play activity (Bailey et al. 1995; Corbin and Pangrazi 2002). Plan multiple activities with rest periods to provide variety and simulate children's natural play pattern. To regulate intensity, engage children in moderate to vigorous activity instead of using target heart rates. Provide adequate rest periods as intensity

TABLE 3.1   FITT Guidelines Applied to Aerobic Fitness

	Children (5-12 yr)
Frequency	• Developmentally appropriate physical activity on all or most days of the week • Several bouts of physical activity lasting 15 min or more daily
Intensity	• Mixture of moderate and vigorous intermittent activity • Moderate = low-intensity games (hopscotch, four square), low activity positions (goalie, outfielders), some chores, yard work • Vigorous = games involving running, chasing, playing sports (level 2 of activity pyramid)
Time	• Accumulation of at least 60 min, and up to several hours of activity • Up to 50% of accumulated minutes should be accumulated in bouts of 15 min or more
Type	• Variety of activities • Activities should be selected from the first three levels of the activity pyramid • Continuous activity should not be expected for most children

National Association for Sport and Physical Education (2004). *Physical activity for children: A statement of guidelines for children ages 5-12,* 2nd ed. Reston, VA: Author.

increases. NASPE (2004a, p. 5) offers this definition of moderate physical activity: "Activities of moderate intensity can be performed for relatively long periods of time without fatigue." The authors suggest games like hopscotch and four-square, low-activity positions such as goalie or outfield in softball, brisk walking, bike riding, and some chores and housework. They define vigorous physical activity as "movement that expends more energy or is performed at a higher intensity than brisk walking. Some forms of vigorous activity, such as running, can be done for relatively long periods of time while others may be so vigorous (e.g., sprinting) that frequent rests are necessary" (p. 5). Refer to *Physical Education for Lifelong Fitness: The Physical Best Teacher's Guide, Second Edition,* chapter 5, "Aerobic Fitness" for more information about intensity.

Training Methods for Aerobic Fitness

The three main training methods for developing and maintaining aerobic fitness are continuous training, interval training, and circuit training.

- Continuous training is the same activity performed over an extended period. We rarely observe this type of activity in children. Fartlek, a modification of continuous training, intersperses periods of increased intensity with continuous activity over varying natural terrain. This type of activity can be modified and used at all grade levels. Fartlek is especially good in exploratory activities at the primary grades and in station or circuit training.

- Interval training involves alternating short bursts of activity with rest periods. Young children naturally engage in this type of activity.

- Circuit training involves several different activities, allowing you to vary the intensity or type of activity as children move from station to station. Circuit training is an excellent method for creating variety and stimulating student motivation.

Motor Skill Development Through Aerobic Fitness

Do not underestimate the importance of skill development, especially at the elementary level. Physical Best activities provide many opportunities to address motor skills during aerobic fitness activities.

Use caution with children during activity periods, because children respond to exercise differently than adults do (Bar-Or 1993, 1994; Zwiren 1988; Rowland 1996). You should give special consideration when manipulating the principles of training and the FITT Guidelines. Include frequent rest periods, be aware of very hot, humid weather, and take extra precautions with elementary school children.

As children become more active you will want to provide information to reduce the risk of injury or illness that may lead to periods of inactivity. The information will be especially valuable when children leave your physical education program and continue to be active after school or in the community. Observe the following safety guidelines:

- Supervise the program closely and individualize the activity.
- Explain rules clearly and insist that students follow them
- Have students wear protective clothing and gear appropriate for the sport, including
  - proper shoes for the activity,
  - helmets for cycling and other sports, and
  - light clothing in the heat.

- Obtain medical information concerning preexisting conditions.

- Minimize exposure to the sun and heat by using shaded space or by having children wear sunscreen and hats.

- Recognize that exercise or activity on very hot and humid days or very cold days may increase health risks. Children have low tolerance to exercise under these conditions (Bar-Or and Malina 1995) because they

  - have a large surface area per unit of mass,

  - sweat at a lower rate,

  - have high metabolic heat production, and

  - take longer to acclimate to hot environments.

- Recognize signs and symptoms of heat illness or cold injury and do what you can to lessen the health risk.

  - Provide plenty of cool water, shade, and rest periods, and reduce intensity of activity.

  - Have students wear layered clothing and limit exposure to cold.

  - When necessary, conduct class indoors to limit exposure to air pollution.

Physical Best provides you and your students with the knowledge, skills, values, and confidence to engage in physical activity now and in the future through enjoyable activities.

Aerobic Fitness Newsletter

Use the Aerobic Fitness Newsletter (located on the CD-ROM) to introduce, reinforce, and extend the concepts behind developing and maintaining good aerobic fitness. The following are ways that you might use this tool:

- Send the newsletter home as a parent-involvement tool during a miniunit focusing on aerobic fitness.

- Use the newsletter to help you feature aerobic fitness as the "Health-Related Fitness Component of the Month."

- Introduce the activity ideas as a whole-group task. Ask students to choose one activity to perform outside class in the next week. They should report their progress through a log, journal, a parent's signature on the newsletter, or other means.

- Validate and promote student involvement in physical activity outside class time and the school setting.

- Among students who can read, promote reading to learn across your curriculum, further supporting the elementary school mission.

- Use the newsletter as a model or springboard to create your own newsletter, tailored specifically to your students' needs.

Feel free to use the Aerobic Fitness Newsletter in a way that helps you teach more effectively to the specific needs of your students and their parents.

Activities

Chapter 3 Activities Grid

Activity number	Activity title	Activity page	Concept	Primary	Intermediate	Reproducible (on CD-ROM)
3.1	Red Light, Green Light	23	Definition	•		Red, Green, and Yellow Light Cards
3.2	Taking Your Heart Rate	25	Definition		•	Taking Your Heart Rate Station Task Cards
						Taking Your Heart Rate Task Sheet
3.3	Fitness Scavenger Hunt	27	Health benefits		•	Health Benefit Checklist
						Health Benefit Picture Cards
						Color Sequence Cards
3.4	Artery Avengers	30	Health benefits	•		Artery Avenger Assessment Sheet
3.5	Benefit Pickup	32	Health benefits	•		Aerobic Fitness Health Benefit Cards
						Aerobic Fitness Health Benefits Poster
3.6	On Your "Spot," Get Set, Go!	34	Warm-up and cool-cown	•		Locomotor Cards
						Warm-Up and Cool-Down Display Cards
3.7	You Should Be Dancing	37	Warm-up and cool-down		•	Dance Step Cards
						Dance Step Descriptions
3.8	Aerobic Activity Picture Chart	39	Frequency	•		Aerobic Activity Picture Chart
3.9	Aerobic Fitness Activity Log	41	Frequency		•	Aerobic Fitness Activity Log
						Activities Goal Contract
3.10	Animal Locomotion	43	Intensity	•		Animal Locomotion Task Cards
3.11	Jumping Frenzy	45	Intensity		•	Jumping Frenzy Instruction Cards
3.12	Pace, Don't Race	47	Time	•		Locomotor, Direction, and Pathway Signs
3.13	Healthy Heart Hoedown	49	Time		•	Dance Cue Cards
3.14	Healthy Heart Tag	51	Type, or specificity	•		Healthy Heart Tag Signs
3.15	You're My Type	53	Type, or specificity		•	You're My Type Instruction Card
3.16	Aerobic FITT Log	55	Progession		•	Aerobic FITT Log
						Aerobic FITT Log Worksheet

3.1 Red Light, Green Light

PRIMARY LEVEL

Aerobic means "with oxygen." The heart and lungs of an aerobically fit person send oxygen and fuel (nutrients) to the muscles so that the person can exercise for longer periods of time.

PURPOSE

- Students will understand that the heart, lungs, and muscles work together when performing aerobic activities.
- Students will engage in sustained physical activity that causes an increase in heart rate and breathing rate.

RELATIONSHIP TO NATIONAL STANDARDS

Physical Education Standard 4: The student achieves and maintains a health-enhancing level of physical fitness.

Health Education Standard 3: The student will demonstrate the ability to practice health-enhancing behaviors and reduce health risks.

EQUIPMENT

Upbeat music

PROCEDURE

1. Ask students to state what red, green, and yellow traffic lights mean. Explain that today they are going to imagine that they are cars. They will follow the traffic lights to help them exercise their hearts. Review or teach students how to find their heart rates. Explain that raising the heart rate through physical activity is good for their hearts. Mention that eating and drinking enough fluid are healthy for the body, good for the heart, and help supply fuel/energy for the activity. In today's lesson the Green-Light Card means "Go," and students should perform the locomotor skill. The Yellow-Light Card means "Slow down." Students walk because they are running out of fuel (oxygen, food, and liquid). The Red-Light Card means "Stop." The car is out of fuel (oxygen, food, and water), so students must check their heart rates by putting a hand over the heart. Have students check their heart rates before beginning the activity.

2. Have students find a spot in the activity area.

Reproducible

- Red, Green, and Yellow Light Cards (print on red, green, and yellow paper to add to the visual effect)

STOP
Your muscles have run out of fuel! Is your heart beating fast or slow?

Activity 3.1 Red, Green, and Yellow Light Cards
From *Physical Best activity guide: Elementary level*, 2nd edition, by NASPE, 2005, Champaign, IL: Human Kinetics.

3. Flash the Green-Light Card. Choose a locomotor skill with which to move. Have the students perform the locomotor skill for 30 seconds.

4. Flash the Yellow-Light Card to signal students to slow down and walk.

5. Finally, flash the Red-Light Card to signal students to stop. Have each student place one hand over the heart and use the other hand to demonstrate the heartbeat (by opening and closing the hand).

6. When students have felt their heart rates, flash the Green-Light Card and increase the activity time (from 30 to 60 seconds).

7. Repeat the yellow and red lights and then have students check for increased heart rates. Ask, "Is it faster?" Repeat the activity until they see that that the body is using oxygen, food, and fuel when it performs activity.

TEACHING HINTS

▨ Make sure that students have a general understanding of how to feel the heart rate by placing a hand on the chest. You can play this game at the beginning of the year to teach stop and start commands.

▨ Ask the art teacher to have students draw their own cars and demonstrate how aerobic fitness is like a car.

SAMPLE INCLUSION TIPS

▨ Create task cards specifically for students using wheelchairs or who need other types of modification. Suggested task cards include: moving in various pathways; lifting weights; using stretch bands.

▨ You can voice the color of card and locomotor skill for students with a visual impairment.

ASSESSMENT

▨ Have students tell what body parts help them most in being active over a long period (heart and lungs).

▨ While students walk on the yellow light, have students name aerobic activities they participate in outside of school.

3.2 Taking Your Heart Rate

INTERMEDIATE LEVEL

Aerobic means "with oxygen." **Aerobic fitness** is the ability of the heart, lungs, and muscles to perform activity over a sustained period. The heart rate represents how fast the heart pumps blood (which carries oxygen) through the body. As the body requires more oxygen to be transported to the muscles, the heart beats faster and the person breathes harder.

PURPOSE

- Students will understand that physical activity increases the heart rate and the circulation of fuels through the body.
- Students will know the definition of heart rate and the significance it has in physical activity.
- Students will understand the effect of different types and intensities of aerobic activity on heart rate.

RELATIONSHIP TO NATIONAL STANDARDS

Physical Education Standard 4: The student achieves and maintains a health-enhancing level of physical fitness.

Health Education Standard 3: The student will demonstrate the ability to practice health-enhancing behaviors and reduce health risks.

EQUIPMENT

- Heart rate monitors (if available) or a clock with a second hand
- Equipment for a circuit of station activities that require:
  - different levels of aerobic fitness (for example, sports skills such as dribbling a basketball or soccer ball)
  - recreational activities such as jumping rope or pretending to in-line skate or ice skate

Reproducibles

- Taking Your Heart Rate Station Task Cards (available on CD-ROM or develop your own)
- Taking Your Heart Rate Task Sheets, one per student

Dribble a Basketball or Soccer Ball

Dribble across the gym and back.

Control the Ball!

What is your six-second heart rate?

Activity 3.2 Taking Your Heart Rate Station Task Cards
From *Physical Best activity guide: Elementary level*, 2nd edition, by NASPE, 2005, Champaign, IL: Human Kinetics

---

Name: _____ Class: _____ Date: _____

Activity 3.2
Taking Your Heart Rate
Task Sheet

Activity	6 second pulse
Dribble a Basketball or Soccer Ball	
Jump Rope	
Skate	
Cross-Country Ski	
Power Walk	
Volley a Ball	
Aerobic Step	
Free Choice Muscular Activity	
Free Choice Stretching Activity	
Surf the Internet	
Clean Your Room	

Activity 3.2 Taking Your Heart Rate Task Sheet
From *Physical Best activity guide: Elementary level*, 2nd edition, by NASPE, 2005, Champaign, IL: Human Kinetics

- outdoor activities such as mimicking cross-country skiing (use carpet strips and dowel rods with rubber tips) or power walking
- pretending to be at a beach by tossing or volleying a beach ball or volleyball
- structured fitness activities such as aerobic stepping, muscular fitness or flexibility exercises
- include stations that depict working conditions that are sedentary such as working at a computer or surfing the Internet and jobs that are more active such as cleaning your room

▓ Pencils

▓ Prerecorded music track and player (optional)

PROCEDURE

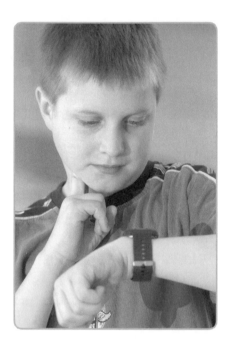

1. Define aerobic fitness. Brainstorm a list of aerobic activities. Explain that today students will be collecting information on how strenuous various activities are by checking and recording their heart rates after each activity. Review how to take an accurate heart rate.

2. Perform a group warm-up.

3. Divide students into the same number of small groups as you have stations.

4. Have students perform each task-card activity for one minute at each station and record their heart rates on a Taking Your Heart Rate Task Sheet.

5. Signal students to rotate to the next activity.

6. Discuss differences in heart rates for the types of activities performed.

TEACHING HINTS

A prerecorded music track makes this activity more enjoyable. Every time the music stops, students find their heart rates and record their scores. When the music starts, they move to the next station.

SAMPLE INCLUSION TIPS

▓ Change size and color of equipment as needed.

▓ Use tactile balls or deflated balloon or beach ball, audible balls, Nerf Frisbees, rubber rings, stretch bands, and light weights as needed.

▓ Use poly spots to create a pattern for students to hop through.

ASSESSMENT

▓ Have students write a definition of aerobic fitness.

▓ Ask students to list activities from today's lesson that were aerobic.

▓ Have students work in small groups to design new stations for aerobic and nonaerobic activities.

▓ Have a group of students modify a game or sport-skill drill to increase aerobic activity and therefore raise heart rates.

3.3 Fitness Scavenger Hunt

INTERMEDIATE LEVEL

Health benefits—Aerobic activities done often over time will benefit the body in many ways.

PURPOSE

Students will be able to list the benefits of aerobic fitness.

RELATIONSHIP TO NATIONAL STANDARDS

Physical Education Standard 4: The student achieves and maintains a health-enhancing level of physical fitness.

EQUIPMENT

- 24 to 32 objects, such as cones (all the same color) to hide crayons and cards under
- 3 to 4 eight-packs of colored crayons
- Checker or similar-sized object, one per team
- Hula hoops, one per team

PROCEDURE

1. Place hoops around the activity space, one per team. Place a Color Sequence Card in each hoop, with a checker or a similar-sized object on the top color of each card to be used as a marker by the students to keep track of where they are on the card.

Reproducibles

- Health Benefit Checklist, one per group
- Health Benefit Picture Cards to hide under cones (health benefit on one side of card and exercise on the reverse side of card)
- Color Sequence Cards, one per group

2. Scatter cones or other objects on playing field, and hide one Health Benefit Picture Card under each object, along with a crayon.

3. Put class into teams of three. Give each team a Health Benefit Checklist and assign each team a hoop as their starting point.

4. Have students check their heart rates before beginning the activity, and ask them to respond to how they think their heart rates might change during the activity.

5. Explain to students that there are benefits to aerobic exercise. Hold up an additional set of the Health Benefit Picture Cards, explain them and tell the students that they will be hunting for these benefits today. Explain that when they find the card, there will be an exercise on the opposite side of the card for them to perform.

6. Tell the students that they will also be hunting for specific colors of crayons, hidden with the Health Benefit Picture Cards.

7. Ask the teams to observe what color their marker (checker) is on and tell them that this is the first crayon color they should find. When they find that color of crayon, they will also find a Health Benefit Picture Card with it.

8. With the crayon that they find, the students will check off the health benefit picture on their Health Benefit Checklist that matches the one on their Health Benefit Picture Card, do 10 repetitions of the exercise on the back of that card, and return the card and crayon to the hiding place.

9. The team should run back to their station, and move their marker down to the next color. They then follow the same procedure as above–starting with step 7.

10. Students continue until the team has completed their color list, or until the end of a predetermined time.

11. Have students recheck their heart rates. Ask them to compare this to the start of the activity.

12. Relate working the heart to the health benefits gained. Discuss possible reasons for some teams having more colors than others (speed, fitness level, luck with finding colors, remembering where colors are located, and so on). Explain that those who did not find as many may have been working their hearts just as hard or harder as those who found more, depending on many factors, especially their individual fitness levels.

13. Remind students that the health benefits of aerobic fitness include a stronger heart, more energy, and a feeling of well-being. Mention that they need to participate in aerobic activities regularly over time to gain the benefits (see also the Aerobic Fitness Activity Picture Chart activity beginning on page 39 or the Aerobic Fitness Activity Log activity on page 41).

TEACHING HINTS

■ If desired, signal students to change the locomotor skill that they are using every 30 to 60 seconds.

■ To make the activity more challenging, place additional objects/cones around that have nothing hidden under them.

■ Monitor class and schedule rest breaks as needed and provide options for varying intensity (such as power walking between cones and hoops).

SAMPLE INCLUSION TIP

Students with limited mobility can seek fewer colors or colors that have been strategically placed closer to them.

ASSESSMENT

■ Direct the class in listing the health benefits of aerobic fitness, either by recall or by recognition by holding up the Benefits Cards.

■ When gauging effort, a look at the index cards will show something about how well each set of partners did, but keep in mind that less-fit students may work harder than more-fit students but still find fewer colors.

3.4 Artery Avengers

PRIMARY LEVEL

Health benefits—Physical activity helps clear fat from arteries (tubes through which blood flows), which helps keep your heart healthy.

PURPOSE

- Students will learn that too much fat will clog the arteries.
- Students will learn that moderate physical activity can help keep the heart and blood vessels healthy.

RELATIONSHIP TO NATIONAL STANDARDS

Physical Education Standard 4: The student achieves and maintains a health-enhancing level of physical fitness.

Health Education Standard 1: The student will comprehend concepts related to health promotion and disease prevention.

EQUIPMENT

- Soft balls (fats)–yarn balls, paper balls, and so on
- Hula hoops (arteries)
- Cones
- Frisbees (shields)

PROCEDURE

1. Explain how blood flows through our arteries (hoops) and how too much fat (yarn balls) in our foods, over the long term, can cause the arteries to clog. Remind students that activity can reduce the amount of fat in the arteries. Explain that the more active you are in the game, the less fat (yarn balls) will collect in your team's arteries (hoops).

2. Divide the students into two groups.

3. Line up cones in the middle of a room to divide the room into two halves. Tell students not to cross over the line. Place the hula hoops (arteries) in the back of each half. Place the yarn balls (fat) randomly around on the floor.

4. Students throw one yarn ball at a time across the room to the opposite hula hoops, trying to fill their opponents' hula hoops with fat balls.

5. Once fat balls are in hoops, students cannot take them out.

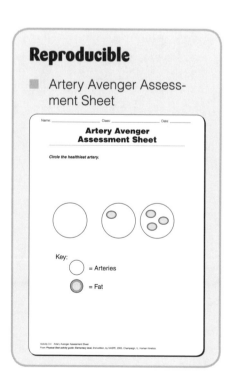

Reproducible

- Artery Avenger Assessment Sheet

6. The game continues until you have a good example of fat balls in hoops to have a discussion—remember that they need some fat to be healthy!

7. Reset the activity.

8. For the second round, select students to act as artery avengers in a ratio of three avengers to six hoops. This ratio should provide some challenge and allow room to move safely about. Artery avengers can block yarn balls (fats) from entering the hoop with a Frisbee, which they should hold like a shield. Tell the students that the shields represent physical activity, to help keep fat from building in the arteries. The avengers may roll out balls that did not land in a hoop to their teammates so that they may throw them.

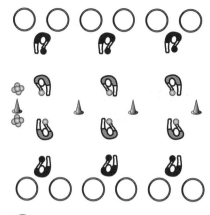

key: ⬭ - hula hoops - arteries
◦ - fleece balls - fat
● - frisbee - shields against fat

TEACHING HINTS

▨ Students should be made aware of the fact that some fat is essential for a healthy body.

▨ Assign students to make and bring a paper ball to class for this activity.

▨ If you have colored Frisbees, you could name them. For example, green represents vegetables, blue represents water, and red represents increased blood flow from exercise. This adaptation adds teaching the role of proper nutrition in maintaining heart health, in addition to physical activity.

SAMPLE INCLUSION TIPS

▨ Designate a safe play area specifically designed for the student(s) with disabilities.

▨ For students with limited mobility, designate a peer helper to help pick up the balls.

ASSESSMENT

▨ Through discussion at the end of activity, have students identify the hula hoops (arteries) that have too much fat. The students should identify hoops largely filled with fat as unhealthy. Those with just a few balls or no balls are okay.

▨ Have students fill out the Artery Avenger Assessment Sheet. Ask students to circle the healthiest artery. The correct answer is the artery with no plaque buildup.

3.5 Benefit Pickup

PRIMARY LEVEL

Health Benefits—Having aerobic fitness helps you learn better, enjoy life, and feel good. Physical activity encourages your heart to beat stronger, your lungs to breathe better, and your muscles to grow stronger.

PURPOSE

- Students will understand the benefits of having aerobic fitness.
- Students will understand the role of physical activity in increasing the ability of the lungs to take in more oxygen and the ability of the heart to beat stronger.

RELATIONSHIP TO NATIONAL STANDARDS

Physical Education Standard 4: The student achieves and maintains a health-enhancing level of physical fitness.

Health Education Standard 3: The student will demonstrate the ability to practice health-enhancing behaviors and reduce health risks.

EQUIPMENT

- Large containers (hoops, buckets, and the like)
- Any medium-paced music

PROCEDURE

1. Brainstorm with students about the benefits of aerobic exercise. Read the Aerobic Fitness Health Benefit Cards to them to introduce the activity.

2. Place the Aerobic Fitness Health Benefit Cards in a central location at each end of the activity area (in containers, hoops, or the like). As an alternative to using the cards, you can write out the benefits on popsicle sticks or tongue depressors and use those instead.

Reproducibles

- Aerobic Fitness Health Benefit Cards
- Aerobic Fitness Health Benefits Poster

Healthy Heart

Activity 3.5 Aerobic Fitness Health Benefit Cards
From *Physical Best activity guide: Elementary level*, 2nd edition, by NASPE, 2005, Champaign, IL: Human Kinetics.

Healthy Breathing

Activity 3.5 Aerobic Fitness Health Benefit Cards
From *Physical Best activity guide: Elementary level*, 2nd edition, by NASPE, 2005, Champaign, IL: Human Kinetics.

Aerobic Fitness Health Benefits

- **Strengthens the heart** (lower resting and working heart rate, faster recovery)
- **Decreases blood pressure**
- **Strengthens muscles and bones**
- **Increases energy** (to play longer)
- **Allows performance of more work with less effort** (carry my toys without becoming tired or needing help)
- **Reduces stress and tension** (get along better with others)
- **Enhances appearance and feeling of well-being; improves quality of life**
- **Improves ability to learn** (get homework done faster)
- **Promotes healthy body composition**
- **Increases self-confidence and self-esteem** (greater social opportunities)
- **Enhances sleep**
- **Improves lipid profile**
- **Weight control**

Activity 3.5 Aerobic Fitness Health Benefits Poster
From *Physical Best activity guide: Elementary level*, 2nd edition, by NASPE, 2005, Champaign, IL: Human Kinetics.

3. Have the students begin moving clockwise or counterclockwise around the activity area using various locomotor patterns. Play music.

4. Every time they pass a container, have them pick up an Aerobic Fitness Health Benefit Card. At the end of the activity (two or three minutes), discuss the benefits listed on the cards or sticks.

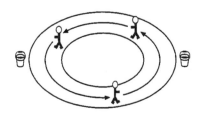

TEACHING HINTS

■ Encourage students to move at a pace that is best for them. Spend adequate time introducing the concepts of health benefits resulting from aerobic fitness before beginning the activity.

■ Develop a bulletin board with the caption "X (school name) Kids Are Active Kids." For display, have students bring in pictures of themselves in their favorite aerobic activities at home, in school, and in the community.

■ Bring in a model or a poster of the heart and discuss what is a healthy heart and cardiovascular system.

SAMPLE INCLUSION TIPS

■ Peer tutor/buddy system would work well with this activity.

■ Raise level of containers if necessary.

ASSESSMENT

■ Have students identify the health benefits that they learned in the activity.

■ Have students share with another class member what health benefits they picked up.

3.6 On Your "Spot," Get Set, Go!

PRIMARY LEVEL

A **warm-up** prepares your heart, lungs, and muscles for activity by slowly increasing blood flow and body temperature. Warming up will help keep you from injuring your muscles. A **cool-down** brings your body slowly back to normal temperature and returns blood flow to normal.

PURPOSE

- Students will understand the importance of warming up before an activity and cooling down after an activity.
- Students will grasp which activities build gradually on others for a warm-up and which descend in intensity from others for a cool-down.

RELATIONSHIP TO NATIONAL STANDARDS

Physical Education Standard 2: The student demonstrates understanding of movement concepts, principles, strategies, and tactics as they apply to the learning and performance of physical activities.

Health Education Standard 1: The student will comprehend concepts related to health promotion and disease prevention.

EQUIPMENT

- One spot for each student (use any, or a combination of, hula hoops, poly spots or carpet squares, and so on)
- Upbeat music with player (use a remote or timed recording to signal activity phases)
- One crayon per student

Reproducibles

- Locomotor Cards
- Warm-Up and Cool-Down Display Cards

Walk

Activity 3.6 Locomotor Cards
From *Physical Best activity guide: Elementary level*, 2nd edition, by NASPE, 2005, Champaign, IL: Human Kinetics.

Warm-Up

Activity 3.6 Warm-Up and Cool-Down Display Cards
From *Physical Best activity guide: Elementary level*, 2nd edition, by NASPE, 2005, Champaign, IL: Human Kinetics.

Slide

Activity 3.6 Locomotor Cards
From *Physical Best activity guide: Elementary level*, 2nd edition, by NASPE, 2005, Champaign, IL: Human Kinetics.

Cool-Down

Activity 3.6 Warm-Up and Cool-Down Display Cards
From *Physical Best activity guide: Elementary level*, 2nd edition, by NASPE, 2005, Champaign, IL: Human Kinetics.

PROCEDURE

1. Ask or explain to students what an appropriate warm-up is. Discuss appropriate cool-downs as well.

2. Help students organize the Locomotor Cards in the correct order for warming up gradually (post below the Warm-Up Display Card as follows: walk, slide, gallop, skip, jog, jump).

3. All students start in scattered formation, each standing at his or her spot.

4. Take a resting heart rate check by having students put their hands over their hearts and show each heart beat by moving the other hand.

5. When the music starts, have students perform a designated locomotor movement between the spots. Begin with walking.

© Human Kinetics

6. When the music stops, students must find a spot and check their heart rates.

7. Continue in the proper warm-up order: slide, gallop, skip, jog, and then jump.

8. Pause the movement and ask students to tell you what a cool-down is and in what order they should do the activities.

9. Repeat the activity in reverse order: jump, jog, skip, gallop, slide, and walk.

10. End with stretching, mentioning it as an additional way to finish cooling down after intense aerobic fitness activity. Have students take a final heart rate to determine if they have slowed their heart rates.

TEACHING HINTS

- If using hula hoops as spot markers, remind students to carefully move around the hoops, and not to step on them.

- Remind them to look for spacing while they are moving. When they move into a hoop or onto a spot, they must not push.

- Help students apply the knowledge. Brainstorm other activities that they can use in an appropriate order to create an aerobic fitness warm-up or cool-down. For example, for a warm-up they could do a dance step slowly, a dance step at moderate speed, and then a dance step quickly. For a cool-down, they could do a dance step quickly, a dance step at moderate speed, and then a dance step slowly. Listen to determine whether students grasp the concept of gradually increasing intensity to warm up and gradually decreasing intensity to cool down.

SAMPLE INCLUSION TIPS

- Have students who are hearing impaired watch other students. When the other students stop, the student with the impairment should stop.

- Use a peer guide for a student with a visual impairment.

ASSESSMENT

- Ask the class to define warm-up and cool-down again.

- Ask questions about locomotor skills and how they relate to the heart. For example, ask, "How does jogging change heart rate compared with walking? How does skipping change heart rate compared with jumping?" Relate answers to appropriate order of activities in warm-ups and cool-downs.

- Observe students checking heart rates and ask them for information on heart rate checks to facilitate this aspect of learning.

- Ask students to judge their own performance by asking questions such as, "Were you able to increase your heart rate gradually through the warm-up?" and, "Were you able to lower your heart rate a lot by the end of the cool-down?" To answer, students can give you a thumbs-up or thumbs-down.

3.7

You Should Be Dancing

INTERMEDIATE LEVEL

A **warm-up** prepares your heart, lungs, and muscles for activity by slowly increasing blood flow and body temperature. Warming up will help keep you from injuring your muscles. A **cool-down** slowly brings your body back to normal temperature and the blood flow back to normal.

PURPOSE

Students will understand why a warm-up and cool-down are important in aerobic activity and how to do both properly.

RELATIONSHIP TO NATIONAL STANDARDS

Dance Education Standard 6: The student makes connections between dance and healthful living.

Physical Education Standard 6: The student values physical activity for health, enjoyment, challenge, self-expression, and/or social interaction.

EQUIPMENT

Music

PROCEDURE

1. Review the importance of and rules for warming up and cooling down. Explain that dancing is an excellent way to increase the heart rate, thereby benefiting the heart and warming up the muscles.

2. Scatter the Dance Step Cards around the activity area. To emphasize the concept of warm-up and cool-down, place activity cards that describe dance steps

Reproducibles

■ Dance Step Cards, laminated

■ Dance Step Descriptions

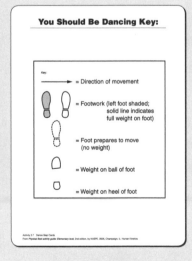

Reprinted, by permission, from Bennett, J.P., and Coughenour Riemer, P. 1995. *Rhythmic activities and dance* (Champaign, IL: Human Kinetics), 20-22.

of lower intensity on one side of the activity area and put cards for moves of higher intensity on the other side. For a warm-up, move through the lower-intensity dance steps first. Finish with the higher-intensity movements. Reverse the sequence for a cool-down.

3. Begin the activity by having the students first listen and then clap to the music, to get the beat.

4. Have students skip, jog, or use another locomotor action to travel to a card. Encourage students to perform the traveling actions to the beat of the music.

5. Direct them to perform the steps on the card, sustaining the movement for a period of time, before they move to the next card.

6. Help students cool down at the end of class by dancing as a group using some of the easier steps.

TEACHING HINTS

■ As an alternative to using the dance-step cards provided on the CD-ROM, make a theme out of the steps to use with cross-curricular teaching (for example, coordinate with social studies by using all folk dance steps) or use all line dances, partner dances, all hip-hop steps, and so on to provide variety.

■ Make sure that students know the dance steps from previous lessons or introduce a few before beginning the activity. (For example, teach a new set of steps as a warm-up in lessons leading up to this activity.)

SAMPLE INCLUSION TIPS

■ For students who are hearing impaired, be sure to include the clapping mentioned in the procedure. Both the teacher and students can continue to clap when moving from card to card so that the student who is hearing impaired can maintain the tempo.

■ Students who are hearing impaired can also be helped by the use of a dance ribbon to describe the rhythm of the music by moving the ribbon fast or slow.

■ Have students who have difficulty with the dance steps dance to a slower beat.

ASSESSMENT

■ Have students explain the reasons why warming up and cooling down benefit the body.

■ Discuss the differences between performing the lower-intensity steps and the higher-intensity steps. How did their heart rates feel (lower or higher)? How did their muscles feel (cooler or warmer)?

3.8 Aerobic Activity Picture Chart

PRIMARY

Frequency is how many days per week you do an aerobic activity. Being active three or four days a week is good, but doing some form of activity most days of the week is best.

PURPOSE

Students will understand and demonstrate how many days each week they should perform aerobic activity.

RELATIONSHIP TO NATIONAL STANDARDS

Physical Education Standard 3: The student participates regularly in physical activity.

Health Education Standard 3: The student will demonstrate the ability to practice health-enhancing behaviors and reduce health risks.

EQUIPMENT

Whatever equipment is necessary to perform an aerobic activity.

PROCEDURE

1. After students participate in a class activity that works on their aerobic fitness, explain that to have healthy hearts they need to engage in physical activity on all or most days of the week. Have the students brainstorm a list of activities that raise their heart rates. Encourage them to use examples from outside physical education class.

2. Pass out the Aerobic Activity Picture Chart, explain how to fill it out, and ask students to work with their parents at home to fill it out for one to two weeks.

TEACHING HINTS

- Encourage students to find different ways to stay active. Give them examples that fit the opportunities in their community.

- Construct a bulletin board with hand-drawn or magazine pictures of the different activities that the students found to do.

- Have a family day in physical education when family members join students in activities that the family can do at home to keep in shape.

- You may want to complete a chart to show the students as an example.

Reproducible

- Aerobic Activity Picture Chart, one per student

Activity 3.8
Aerobic Activity Picture Chart

Circle the activities that you have done in the past week or in a blank space draw another activity that you have done. How many days did you do this activity? If it is more than one, write that number by the picture.

SAMPLE INCLUSION TIPS

- Discuss with each student what physical activities they participate in outside of school.

- Use this activity as an opportunity for diversity training. Have students with disabilities share or demonstrate the activities they participate in outside of school.

ASSESSMENT

- Have students tell you how many days per week they should give their hearts, lungs, and muscles a workout.

- Collect the homework sheet and lead a class discussion on the activities circled and added.

- Have students discuss their favorite aerobic activity with a friend or the class.

© Human Kinetics

3.9 Aerobic Fitness Activity Log

INTERMEDIATE LEVEL

Frequency is how many days per week you should perform aerobic activity to improve your heart rate, breathing rate, and muscle function. You should perform physical activity that you enjoy on all or most days of the week.

PURPOSE

Students will understand and demonstrate how many days each week they should perform aerobic activity.

RELATIONSHIP TO NATIONAL STANDARDS

Physical Education Standard 3: The student participates regularly in physical activity.

Health Education Standard 3: The student will demonstrate the ability to practice health-enhancing behaviors and reduce health risks.

EQUIPMENT

- Whatever equipment is necessary to perform an aerobic activity.
- Pencils

PROCEDURE

1. After students participate in a class activity that works on their aerobic fitness, explain to them that to have healthy hearts they need to engage in physical activity on most days of the week. Have the students brainstorm a list of activities that raise their heart rates. Encourage them to use examples from outside physical education class.

2. Have students fill out and sign an Activity Goals Contract.

3. Pass out the Aerobic Fitness Activity Log, explain how to fill it out, and ask them to work with their parents at home to fill it out for the next one to two weeks.

Reproducibles

- Aerobic Fitness Activity Log (one per student)
- Activities Goal Contract

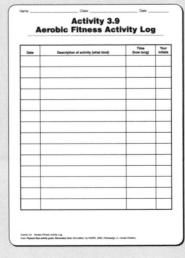

TEACHING HINTS

- Encourage students to find different ways to stay active. Give them examples appropriate for their community.

- The physical education lesson for the day could be stations that depict different activities that students can do on their own. At the end of class, discuss the importance of frequency and challenge them to keep doing activities at home and filling out their activity charts.

- As an extension, have a family day in physical education when family members join students in activities that the family can do at home to keep in shape.

- Consider using the Presidential Active Lifestyle Award (PALA) program as part of this lesson. For information on the PALA, go to www.presidentschallenge.org.

© Human Kinetics

SAMPLE INCLUSION TIPS

- Discuss with each student what physical activities they participate in outside of school.

- Provide parents and students with a list of agencies (departments of parks and recreation or therapeutic recreation programs) that offer a variety of programs for students with disabilities outside of the school environment.

ASSESSMENT

- Have students tell or write a definition of frequency and compare their log to the number of days per week they should participate in aerobic fitness activities.

- Collect the homework sheet and lead a class discussion on activities that the students participate in most frequently.

3.10 Animal Locomotion

PRIMARY LEVEL

Intensity is how hard you work your heart during physical activity. As you work harder, your lungs breathe harder to bring in more oxygen. Your heart beats faster to move the blood through your body to deliver oxygen and nutrients to the muscles. As the blood flow increases, you get hotter and may begin to sweat. To replace the water you lose through sweat, you should drink plenty of water before, during, and after activity.

PURPOSE

- Students will differentiate between movements that are more and less aerobically intense.
- Students will understand that the harder they work, the harder their hearts beat, the faster they breathe, and the hotter their bodies become.
- Students will understand that increasing intensity of an aerobic activity will help strengthen the heart.

RELATIONSHIP TO NATIONAL STANDARDS

Physical Education Standard 4: The student achieves and maintains a health-enhancing level of physical fitness.

Health Education Standard 1: The student will comprehend concepts related to health promotion and disease prevention.

EQUIPMENT

Music or a tambourine

PROCEDURE

1. Explain the concept of intensity. State that today students will be working harder and harder, checking their heart rates to see what their hearts do as they work harder. Ask students why it is important to increase the intensity of an activity (makes the heart stronger and improves the health of your lungs and blood vessels). Have students practice feeling their heart rates by placing one hand over the left side of the chest; this method will give a baseline heart rate to which they may compare their heart rates during the activity. Ask, "What else might your body do when it's working hard?"

2. Direct students to do the following:

   - Move to an open space of the activity area, and move around in general space while being aware of others around them.

Reproducible

- Animal Locomotion Task Cards

Walk like a dog

Activity 3.10 Animal Locomotion Task Cards
From *Physical Best activity guide: Elementary level, 2nd edition*, by NASPE, 2005, Champaign, IL: Human Kinetics.

43

- Check their heart rates by placing one hand over their hearts. Simulate the heart pumping with the free hand whenever checking heart rate during this activity.
- When you hold up card 1 (walk like a dog), the students should walk for 30 seconds and then check their heart rates.

3. Hold up each of the sequential Animal Locomotion Cards for 30 seconds and have students check their heart and breathing rate between each one.

© Human Kinetics

TEACHING HINTS

- Before beginning the activity, ensure that all students know how to feel their heart rates by placing a hand over the left side of the chest.
- Make sure that students know how to move safely in general space.

SAMPLE INCLUSION TIP

Consider allowing students who will require variations to the locomotor cards the chance to review the cards prior to the lesson so they can think about how they can best complete the tasks in class.

ASSESSMENT

- Ask students what animal movements they thought were the hardest.
- Have students tell you how they can tell that one animal movement varies in intensity from another.

3.11 Jumping Frenzy

INTERMEDIATE LEVEL

Intensity is how hard you do your physical activity. As you work harder, your lungs work harder to bring in more oxygen. Your heart beats faster to move the blood through your body to deliver oxygen and nutrients to the muscles. As the blood flow increases, you get hotter and may begin to sweat. To replace the water you lose through sweat, you should drink plenty of water before, during, and after activity.

PURPOSE

- Students will learn the benefits of good aerobic fitness.
- Students will demonstrate the principle of intensity by participating in a series of jumping activities that vary in intensity.
- Students learn to check their heart rates to monitor the intensity of each activity.

RELATIONSHIP TO NATIONAL STANDARDS

Physical Education Standard 4: The student achieves and maintains a health-enhancing level of physical fitness.

EQUIPMENT

- Cones
- Boom box and CDs of choice
- Jump ropes (to create shapes on floor)

PROCEDURE

1. Set up stations using Jumping Frenzy Instruction Cards on the CD-ROM, or create your own.
2. Remind students of the definition of aerobic fitness and define intensity as it relates to aerobic activity.
3. Have students warm up as a group.
4. Divide the class into groups of two or four. Have each group start at a different station and tell them to go clockwise or counterclockwise.
5. Have students work at each station for 15 seconds and then rotate to the next station.
6. Perform a group cool-down by walking around the activity space while conducting the oral assessment.

Reproducible

- Jumping Frenzy Instruction Cards with instructions for each station

Jump and spin in the air so that you face the opposite direction.

Activity 3.11 Jumping Frenzy Instruction Cards
From *Physical Best activity guide (Elementary level, 2nd edition)*, by NASPE, 2005, Champaign, IL: Human Kinetics.

TEACHING HINTS

- Have one or more stations as a rest stop (could be a water fountain!), depending on the age of the group, fitness level, and duration that you perform the activity.

- Use double-dutch, elastic bands, or jump ropes and adjust the stations for a variation.

- Within a two-week period, see how many ideas the student can come up with for new jumping patterns. Have them practice rope jumping at recess.

- Have small groups of students design a different set of stations using other locomotor activities. Have them name each station game and describe how they can vary the intensity in the activity.

- At the next class meeting, have the students increase the duration of the exercises by increasing the time at each jump station from 15 seconds to 20 seconds. This will increase the intensity and reinforce the teaching of this concept.

SAMPLE INCLUSION TIPS

- Allow students who have trouble turning or jumping the rope to turn the rope at the side and just jump. Or split the rope in half and have them turn the rope and continue to jump. This way they do not need to clear the rope.

- Students in wheelchairs can wheel their chairs back and forth over a line.

ASSESSMENT

- After the activity, ask the group to rate their exertion level using adjectives like light, medium, and hard.

- Ask students which activities were most intense and why.

- Have students state or write a definition of intensity, and an example of how they could change the intensity of the activity (jump higher or lower, jump for a longer or shorter time, and so on).

3.12 Pace, Don't Race

PRIMARY LEVEL

Time is how long you participate in an activity. Children should accumulate at least 60 minutes of physical activity on all or most days of the week and participate in several bouts of physical activity lasting 15 minutes or more each day (NASPE 2004a).

PURPOSE

- Students will be able to identify time as it relates to aerobic fitness.
- Students will understand the importance of pacing themselves to sustain activity over a period of time.

RELATIONSHIP TO NATIONAL STANDARDS

Physical Education Standard 3: The student participates regularly in physical activity.

Health Education Standard 3: The student will demonstrate the ability to practice health-enhancing behaviors and reduce health risks.

EQUIPMENT

Upbeat music

PROCEDURE

1. Have students find their own personal spaces. Explain that to get the most benefit from physical activity, they need to keep moving for at least 15 minutes at a time and pace themselves during the activity. They are going to do this by practicing their locomotor skills.

2. Review the locomotor skills, directions, and pathways, and have everyone practice them.

3. When the music starts, call out a locomotor skill and direction. The students continue to do this skill until you call out a new skill.

4. Throughout the 15-minute time period, vary the locomotor skills, direction, and pathway—holding up the cards, and changing one element at a time.

5. At the end of the activity, point out that what the students just did was only a fraction of the time they need to be moving in a day to keep healthy (a minimum of 60 minutes). Have them brainstorm ways that they can get the rest of the time of activity into their day.

Reproducible

- Locomotor, Direction, and Pathway Signs

Locomotor

Walk

Activity 3.12 Locomotor, Direction, and Pathway Signs
From *Physical Best activity guide: Elementary level*, 2nd edition, by NASPE, 2005, Champaign, IL: Human Kinetics.

Locomotor

Gallop

Activity 3.12 Locomotor, Direction, and Pathway Signs
From *Physical Best activity guide: Elementary level*, 2nd edition, by NASPE, 2005, Champaign, IL: Human Kinetics.

TEACHING HINTS

- Make this activity more enjoyable by using music that includes the locomotor skill in the words of the song (for example, use the Pointer Sisters' song "Jump").
- Switch songs for each locomotor skill.

SAMPLE INCLUSION TIP

Have students with physical disabilities create their own movements related to the various locomotor skills.

ASSESSMENT

© Human Kinetics

- To do a self-assessment, students can see whether they were able to pace themselves to move continuously for a period of at least 5 minutes without stopping.
- Thumbs up or thumbs down—Put your thumb up if you didn't run out of breath and felt like you had the energy to complete the activity until you were told to stop.
- Have students keep a log for a week on the activities they choose. See the activity chart earlier in this chapter for an example of a log (Activity 3.9).

3.13 Healthy Heart Hoedown

INTERMEDIATE LEVEL

Time is how long you participate in an activity. Children should accumulate at least 60 minutes of physical activity on all or most days of the week and participate in several bouts of physical activity lasting 15 minutes or more each day (NASPE 2004a).

PURPOSE

The students will participate in aerobic square dancing to gain an understanding of the time concept of FITT.

RELATIONSHIP TO NATIONAL STANDARDS

Dance Education Standard 1: The student identifies and demonstrates movement elements and skills in performing dance.

Dance Education Standard 6: The student makes connections between dance and healthful living.

EQUIPMENT

- Square dance music, with or without cues
- Music player

PROCEDURE

1. Put students into pairs.

2. Teach basic square dance calls to students; point out that this activity not only teaches them the steps but also serves as a warm-up.

3. Explain to students that practicing these steps will help them raise their heart rates and thus improve their aerobic fitness.

4. Explain or review the concept of time related to FITT. Children should do at least 60 minutes of physical activity on all or most days of the week, at least 15 minutes at a time.

5. Place the Dance Cue Cards in a large circle on the floor, then select those cards coded for pairs. Tell each pair of students to pick a place to start. Tell students that you will now start timing the class to see how many minutes they can add up before the end of class.

6. Direct students in practice of the square dance calls.

7. Tell them you will blow a whistle or stop the music to have them rotate to the next card—and give directions on which way they will rotate.

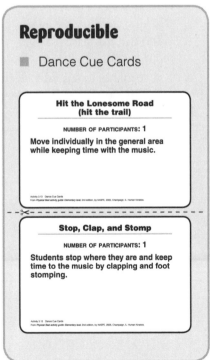

Reproducible

- Dance Cue Cards

Hit the Lonesome Road (hit the trail)

NUMBER OF PARTICIPANTS: 1

Move individually in the general area while keeping time with the music.

Activity 3.13 Dance Cue Cards
From *Physical Best activity guide: Elementary level*, 2nd edition, by NASPE, 2005, Champaign, IL: Human Kinetics.

Stop, Clap, and Stomp

NUMBER OF PARTICIPANTS: 1

Students stop where they are and keep time to the music by clapping and foot stomping.

Activity 3.13 Dance Cue Cards
From *Physical Best activity guide: Elementary level*, 2nd edition, by NASPE, 2005, Champaign, IL: Human Kinetics.

8. During a cool-down, tell the students how long they participated in the activity.

TEACHING HINTS

- When revisiting this activity, also teach the cards coded for singles, groups of four, and all. Follow the same procedure, but periodically call out the additional cards to vary the activity.

- For a change, try using modern music with square dance.

- To extend the activity, have students work in small groups to design original dances.

SAMPLE INCLUSION TIP

Encourage students using wheelchairs to perform to the best of their ability—have a partner assist with moving.

ASSESSMENT

- Have students chant the two-word definition of time ("How Long") and the total time they danced after you started timing them, as they line up to leave the activity area. For example, they can say, "How long? 22 minutes! How long? 22 minutes! How long? 22 minutes!"

- Ask students, "How many more minutes do you need to add today to the number you did in class to make the minimum requirement?" (For example, 60 − 22 = 38 more minutes, before or after class.)

- Ask students to log how many minutes they spend doing activity that improves their aerobic fitness between now and the next class.

- As homework, have students create a clever poster that illustrates time as related to FITT. Display posters to reinforce the concept with peers and younger students.

3.14 Healthy Heart Tag

PRIMARY LEVEL

Type means that certain activities use more oxygen and require you to breathe faster and your heart to beat faster. You must learn to choose activities that strengthen your heart.

PURPOSE

■ Students will identify heart-healthy activities that they enjoy participating in to develop their aerobic fitness.

■ Students will begin to understand how frequency, intensity, and time can influence aerobic fitness.

RELATIONSHIP TO NATIONAL STANDARDS

Physical Education Standard 3: The student participates regularly in physical activity.

Health Education Standard 1: The student will comprehend concepts related to health promotion and disease prevention.

EQUIPMENT NEEDED

■ Segmented music and music player

■ Equipment necessary for activity stations

■ Pinnies for taggers (5)

PROCEDURE

1. Place the Healthy Heart Tag Signs around the perimeter of the activity area.

2. Explain to students that many types of activities can improve aerobic fitness. Go to every activity station and demonstrate the activity.

3. Then describe how to play Healthy Heart Tag: When students are tagged, they should go to a Healthy Heart Tag aerobic activity area of their choosing and participate in the activity listed on the sign. They return to the game when they have completed the activity. Once tagged again, they go to another station. Once they have completed two stations, they become a tagger, politely switching roles with a student who has already been a tagger for a while. (Taggers should wear pinnies or some other simple form of identification, which should be handed over when students switch roles).

Reproducible

■ Healthy Heart Tag Signs

Power Walk

Activity 3.14 Healthy Heart Tag Signs
From *Physical Best activity guide: Elementary level*, 2nd edition, by NASPE, 2005, Champaign, IL: Human Kinetics.

4. Choose three to five students to be taggers.

5. Select a locomotor movement to use for the activity.

6. Because this game is vigorous, use a segmented music tape with rest intervals programmed into the music. During the resting segments, have students feel their pulses to check for increased heart rates. In addition, have them monitor their breathing rates.

7. Change taggers often.

TEACHING HINTS

Make sure that the rest segments on the music tape are long enough for students to check their pulses.

SAMPLE INCLUSION TIP

When a student with a physical disability is a tagger, that student can call out the name of the student they wish to tag. When a student wants to tag a student with a disability, that student should call out the student with a disability's name, and then walk heel to toe until they catch up with the student they want to tag.

ASSESSMENT

■ Ask the students to name several examples of aerobic activities.

■ Ask students how aerobic activity is good for the body.

3.15 You're My Type

INTERMEDIATE LEVEL

Type means that certain activities use more oxygen and require you to breathe faster and your heart to beat faster. You must learn to choose activities that strengthen your heart.

PURPOSE

■ Students will understand that they must select certain types of activities to develop, increase, or maintain aerobic fitness.

■ Students will apply this knowledge through participating in a variety of health-related fitness activities and identify which enhance aerobic fitness and which enhance other components instead.

RELATIONSHIP TO NATIONAL STANDARDS

Physical Education Standard 3: The student participates regularly in physical activity.

EQUIPMENT

■ Equipment for 10 to 12 stations, three to four stations to develop aerobic fitness (for example, jump rope, step-ups, jogging), flexibility (for example, triceps stretches, hamstring stretches), and muscular strength and endurance (for example, exercises with resistive exercise bands, triceps push-ups, wall sits)

■ Interval music recording with player

PROCEDURE

1. Place instruction cards at each station.

2. Divide the class into small groups and have them rotate through all stations. Use the interval music recording to signal activity and use silence to signal rotation.

3. After students have rotated through all stations, ask them to identify which were aerobic fitness stations and which were not. (If you use the cards included on the CD-ROM for this activity, the answers will be: jump rope, step-ups, jogging, and 360-degree jump turns). Ask, "Was the activity vigorous? Did it use large muscle groups? Could you keep it up for a long time?"

4. Explain that the aerobic fitness stations featured exercises that develop aerobic fitness. By understanding the kind of activity at each station, students can target specific components of health-related physical fitness and choose appropriate activities outside class that will help them develop aerobic fitness.

Reproducible

■ You're My Type Instruction Cards, one per station

fold

Jump Rope

Activity 3.15   You're My Type Instruction Cards
From *Physical Best activity guide: Elementary level*, 2nd edition, by NASPE, 2005, Champaign, IL: Human Kinetics.

TEACHING HINTS

■ Have students identify what fitness improvement the other stations would help them make. Explain that the exercises at the other stations would allow them to work on other components of health-related physical fitness (flexibility, muscular strength and endurance).

■ Design stations that enhance your current motor-skills unit, such as sport-specific exercises to aid performance in basketball, soccer, softball, and gymnastics.

■ Reduce setup time by creating only one or two stations each for flexibility and muscular strength and endurance (but create three or four stations for aerobic fitness to emphasize it).

■ Revisit this lesson when focusing on type of activity for muscular strength and endurance. Emphasize the relevant health-related physical fitness component instead of aerobic fitness.

■ Note that the more stations you have, the less time students will spend performing aerobic fitness activities. Therefore, the answer to the third question under step 2—Could I keep it up for a long time?—may need to be qualified with "if given the chance."

SAMPLE INCLUSION TIPS

■ Modify station activities as needed.

■ Use red and green flash cards or flags for students with hearing impairments to stop and go.

ASSESSMENT

■ As the class leaves for the day, have each student state one physical activity that develops aerobic fitness. Do not allow two students in a row to state the same activity. If a student is stumped, have him or her wait by the door to hear a few other students and then have him or her repeat one.

■ Ask students to list in their journals three activities that help develop aerobic fitness.

3.16 Aerobic FITT Log

INTERMEDIATE LEVEL

The **overload principle** states that a body system (cardiorespiratory, muscular, or skeletal) must perform at a level beyond normal in order to adapt and improve physiological function and fitness. **Progression** refers to *how* an individual should increase overload. Proper progression involves a gradual increase in the level of exercise that is manipulated by increasing frequency, intensity, or time, or a combination of all three components.

PURPOSE

Students will learn and apply the training principles of progression and overload for aerobic fitness by completing a FITT Log and worksheet.

RELATIONSHIP TO NATIONAL STANDARDS

Physical Education Standard 3: The student participates regularly in physical activity.

Physical Education Standard 4: The student achieves and maintains a health-enhancing level of physical fitness.

Health Education Standard 3: The student will demonstrate the ability to practice health-enhancing behaviors and reduce health risks.

EQUIPMENT

Pencils

PROCEDURE

1. Briefly review the two-word definitions of the aspects of FITT—frequency (how often), intensity (how hard), time (how long), and type (what kind).

Reproducibles

■ Aerobic FITT Log
■ Aerobic FITT Log Worksheet

2. Ask students to offer brief examples of how they have applied the FITT Guidelines to aerobic fitness in previous health-related fitness lessons.

3. Share descriptions of the concepts of progression and overload.

4. Distribute one blank Aerobic FITT Log to each student. Review each category and how it relates to FITT. Outline how students can apply progression and overload as they use this form.

5. Ask class to share aerobic activities they enjoy, and then tell them to choose one and write it on their log.

6. Have the students write their name on their log.

7. Assign students to log the aerobic fitness activity that they perform outside class for one week.

8. Have students fill in week one of the Aerobic FITT Log Worksheets.

9. Guide students in setting goals for progression and overload and write them on the worksheet.

10. At the end of each week meet with the class to discuss their progress and set new goals.

TEACHING TIPS

- Ask students at each class meeting how their logs are coming along.
- Require parent or guardian initials if necessary to encourage participation.
- Ask the school's after-school care providers to provide space, time, and other support for students to add to their logs.
- Tie the *FITNESSGRAM* aerobic assessment along with this activity.

SAMPLE INCLUSION TIP

Help students with special circumstances come up with alternative activities to suit their needs and abilities. You can modify activities suggested earlier in this chapter, provide suggestions for students who must stay indoors because of safety or space constraints, or otherwise help students develop activity ideas that will work for them.

ASSESSMENT

After the month, have students review their logs with you and write about their experience by answering questions such as the following:

- Were you able to safely build up to a higher level of intensity over the course of the month, do the activities more frequently each week, or spend more time doing each activity? Which changes did you make, if any?
- If you were able to make changes, how might the changes have affected your aerobic fitness?

■ If you did not make changes, what might you be able to do differently in the future?

Realize that many factors, such as the child's initial level of fitness and participation (if already high, they may not progress for that reason), and other personal factors may affect the answers to these questions. Keeping this in mind, focus on the assessment as a means to teach and reinforce the concepts of progression and overload.

Muscular Strength and Endurance

Chapter Contents

Although the literature does not offer a clear-cut conclusion about whether children attain health benefits from resistance training similar to those that adults achieve, children can safely improve muscular strength and endurance if they follow appropriate training guidelines. Sothern, Loftin, Suskind, Udall, and Becker (1999) reported findings that the prepubescent child is at increased risk for injury because of a reduction in joint flexibility caused by rapid growth of long bones. Their findings suggest that strength gains may reduce the risk of acute sports injuries and overuse injuries. For more information concerning the principles of training for muscular strength and endurance, refer to *Physical Education for Lifelong Fitness: The Physical Best Teacher's Guide, Second Edition*. This chapter includes several activities for developing muscular strength and endurance in elementary level students.

Defining Muscular Strength and Endurance

Muscular strength is the ability of a muscle or muscle group to exert maximal force against a resistance one time through the full range of motion. A child perceives this as the ability to act independently, or to lift and carry objects without assistance. *Muscular endurance* is the ability of a muscle or muscle group to exert a submaximal force repeatedly over time. Frequently, the activities performed to develop muscular strength also develop some muscular endurance, because many of the activities use the child's own body weight and involve several repetitions. Because separating these two areas of health-related fitness is often difficult, Physical Best suggests that at the elementary level you label your unit as muscular strength and endurance, or muscular fitness.

Potential benefits of resistance training include the following:

- Increased muscular strength (I'm able to push or lift my bike)
- Increased muscular endurance (I'm able to play a long time without my legs getting tired)
- Improvement in aerobic fitness through muscular fitness circuit training (I'm able to play longer without getting tired)
- Prevention of musculoskeletal injury (I will not get hurt as easily or often)
- Improved sports performance (I can help my soccer team by being a better player)
- Reduced risk of fractures in adulthood (builds stronger bones)
- Exercise during the skeletal growth period is better for bone development, increasing bone strength and bone growth (builds stronger bones)

Activities found in this chapter will introduce and familiarize elementary level students with these benefits.

Teaching Guidelines for Muscular Strength and Endurance

As with each area of health-related fitness, the principles of training (progression, overload, specificity, regularity, and individuality) should be incorporated into the activity. Manipulate the FITT Guidelines based on the age of the child. Keep in mind that chronological age may not match physiological maturation. Note that the guidelines in table 4.1 are only guiding principles for development of muscular strength and endurance. Kraemer and Fleck (1993) suggest the following guidelines for resistance exercise:

- **7 years old and younger**—Introduce the child to basic exercises with little or no weight; develop the concept of a training session; teach exercise techniques; progress from body weight calisthenics, partner exercise, and lightly resisted exercises; and keep volume low.

■ **8 to 10 years old**—Gradually increase the number of exercises; practice exercise technique in all lifts; start gradual progressive loading of exercises; keep exercises simple; gradually increase training volume; and carefully monitor toleration of exercise stress.

■ **11 to 13 years old**—Teach all basic exercise techniques; continue progressive loading of each exercise; emphasize exercise techniques; and use little or no resistance when introducing more advanced exercises.

Training Methods for Muscular Strength and Endurance

A child with no resistance training experience should begin at the previous level, regardless of age, and move to the next level as he or she develops exercise tolerance, skill, and understanding of the lifting techniques.

Several recommendations or position stands are available for resistance training (not weight lifting; see the *Physical Education for Lifelong Fitness: The Physical Best Teacher's Guide,* Second Edition) to provide guidance in developing children's resistance training programs (ACSM 2000; AAP 2001; Hass et al. 2001; NSCS 1985). Use these guidelines to assist you in developing a safe and developmentally appropriate muscular strength and endurance unit.

Beginning students, especially elementary students, should engage primarily in circuit training using their own body weight, partners, or light medicine balls. The volume should be low and the intensity very low (Bompa 2000). Children should try performing reverse curl-ups or the lowering phase of the push-up (holding the lower position) if they have difficulty performing the regular curl-up or push-up. Upper elementary students may begin to participate in partner-resisted exercises and resistance band training. Save weight training using machine weights or barbells for postpubescent children.

Motor Skill Development Through Muscular Strength and Endurance Activities

Using the weight room to develop muscular strength and endurance is not always necessary or appropriate. Students may engage in a variety of motor skills to increase muscular strength and endurance. For example, primary students engaged in a tag game may be using

● ●

TABLE 4.1   FITT Guidelines Applied to Muscular Fitness

Ages	9-11 yr [a, b]	12-14 yr [a, b]
Frequency	2-3 times per week	2-3 times per week
Intensity	Very light weight	Light weight
Time	At least 1 set (may do 2 sets) 6-15 reps At least 20-30 min	At least 1 set (may do 3 sets) 6-15 reps At least 20-30 min
Type	Major muscle groups, one exercise per muscle or muscle group	Major muscle groups, one exercise per muscle or muscle group

[a]Modified from AAP (2001). Strength training by children and adolescents (RE0048). *Pediatrics,* 107(6): 1470-1472.

[b]Modified from A.D. Faigenbaum, et al. 1996. Youth resistance training: Position statement paper and literature review. *Strength and Conditioning,* 18(6): 62-75.

locomotor skills such as hopping or skipping that improve muscular strength and endurance of the leg muscles. Older students may enjoy team-building activities that necessitate arm strength for success. Motor-skill development through fitness activity is the perfect area for you to consider the abilities and disabilities of all students. Some are high achievers, others are low achievers, and still others have physical or intellectual disabilities. Provide opportunities for all students to develop physical skills and be successful in your classroom. If a student is severely disabled, you may need to contact someone who specializes in adapted physical education for assistance in developing an individualized education plan. Many of the Physical Best activities either incorporate a variety of motor skills or allow you to create modifications to the activity to address the motor development needs of your students.

Muscular Strength and Endurance Newsletter

Use the Muscular Strength and Endurance Newsletter (located on the CD-ROM) to introduce, reinforce, and extend the concepts behind developing and maintaining good muscular strength and endurance. The following are ways you might consider using this tool:

- Send the newsletter home as a parent-involvement tool during a miniunit focusing on muscular strength and endurance.

- Use the newsletter to help you feature muscular strength and endurance as the "Health-Related Fitness Component of the Month."

- Introduce the activity ideas as a whole-group task. Ask students to choose one activity to perform outside class in the next week. They should report their progress through a log, journal, a parent's signature on the newsletter, or other means.

- Validate and promote student involvement in physical activity outside class time and the school setting.

- Among students who can read, promote reading to learn across your curriculum, further supporting the elementary school mission.

- Use the newsletter as a model or springboard to create your own newsletters, tailored specifically to your students' needs.

- Feel free to use the Muscular Strength and Endurance Newsletter in a way that helps you teach more effectively to the specific needs of your students and their parents.

Chapter 4 Activities Grid

Activity number	Activity title	Activity page	Concept	Primary	Intermediate	Reproducible (on CD-ROM)
4.1	Mix It Up	63	Definition		●	Mix It Up Station Signs
4.2	Muscle Hustle	67	Definition		●	Muscle Hustle Station Signs
						Muscle Hustle Score Sheet
4.3	Talk to the Animals	70	Health benefits	●		Animal Walk Cards
4.4	Sport Roundup	72	Health benefits		●	Sport Roundup Station Signs
						Health Benefit Signs
						Sport Roundup Task Sheet
4.5	Muscular Strength and Endurance Activity Picture Chart	75	Frequency	●		Muscular Strength and Endurance Picture Activity Picture Chart
4.6	Muscular Strength and Endurance Activity Log	77	Frequency		●	Muscular Strength and Endurance Activity Log
4.7	Statue, Statue	79	Intensity	●		Muscle Groups Picture
4.8	Move and Improve Obstacle Course	81	Intensity		●	None
4.9	Time Flies!	85	Time		●	Time Flies! Rep and Set Poster
						Time Flies! Station Signs
						Time Flies! Worksheet
4.10	Muscle Trek	88	Type, or specificity	●		Muscle Trek Planet Signs
4.11	Shuffle and Hustle	90	Type, or specificity		●	Shuffle and Hustle Suit Posters
4.12	Push-Up Curl-Up Challenge	92	Progression		●	Push-Up Challenge Poster
						Curl-Up Challenge Poster
						Push-Up Curl-Up Challenge Log
4.13	Muscular Strength and Endurance FITT Log	95	Progression		●	Muscle Strength and Endurance FITT Log
						Muscle Strength and Endurance FITT Log Worksheet

4.1

Mix It Up

INTERMEDIATE LEVEL

Muscular strength is the ability to move your body or an object as hard as you can once. Muscular strength is the greatest force that a group of muscles can produce. **Muscular endurance** is the ability to move your body or an object repeatedly without getting tired. Most physical activities require both muscular strength and endurance.

PURPOSE

- Students will learn that they need strength to do a task once.
- Students will learn that they need endurance to do a task many times.
- Students will understand that everyone has different muscular strength and endurance levels.

RELATIONSHIP TO NATIONAL STANDARDS

Physical Education Standard 1: The student demonstrates competency in motor skills and movement patterns needed to perform a variety of physical activities.

Physical Education Standard 3: The student participates regularly in physical activity.

Health Education Standard 3: The student will demonstrate the ability to practice health-enhancing behaviors and reduce health risks.

EQUIPMENT

- Four to six scooters
- Six steps
- Cones
- Tape for line
- Agility ladder or poly spots
- Vertical jump wall marks

PROCEDURE

1. Define muscular strength and endurance. Explain that each person is unique in how much muscular strength and endurance he or she has. State that today's activity will show the difference between muscular strength and muscular endurance by using several stations.

Reproducible

- Mix It Up Station Signs (see list of stations in sidebar)

STATION 1
Scooter Push-Away

Sit on your scooter facing the wall. Use one big push with your feet to see how far you can push yourself from the wall.

2. Describe the stations and their purposes. Identify and discuss safety concerns at Scooter Push-Away (station 1).

3. Divide students into eight groups and send one group to each station.

4. Signal students to perform the station activity and remain there until the signal to rotate.

5. Continue to rotate students until every group has visited all eight stations.

Stations for Mix It Up

Note: The stations alternate between muscular strength or power and muscular endurance activities.

Station 1—Scooter Push-Away

Seated on scooter facing the wall, the student pushes off with both feet to see how strong his or her legs are from that one effort (muscular strength).

The push can be measured. Measure several pushes to see which one was the farthest and on which push the student's legs gave the greatest effort.

Station 2—Scooter Travel

Lying face down on the scooter, the student travels from point A to point B in and around cones for a time to experience pulling themselves around with their arms (muscular endurance). (If the surface area of the activity space is not clean and smooth, have students sit on the scooters and push themselves with their feet.)

Station 3—Maximum Vertical Jump

The student stands with his or her side to the wall and performs a maximum vertical jump (muscular strength). The student can attempt a number of jumps to see on which jump the legs were the strongest and how high he or she jumped.

Station 4—Repeating Step-Up

The student faces a step bench and steps up with the right leg—bringing the left knee up, steps down with the left leg and taps down with the right, performs 8 to 15 repetitions on one leg before switching (muscular endurance).

Station 5—Maximum Horizontal Jump (Long Jump)

The student jumps forward (from standing position) one time with maximum strength (muscular strength). The student can repeat the jump a few times to see on which jump the legs were the strongest.

Station 6—Power Jumps

The student jumps from the number one spot on the floor to the center then continues through the numbers (muscular endurance).

Station 7—Mississippi Push-Ups

In a full or modified push-up position, the student lowers themselves to the ground as slowly as possible, counting "1 Mississippi, 2 Mississippi," and so on. The student can rest and then repeat it, trying to increase his or her count (muscular strength).

Station 8—Agility Hops

The student hops through an agility ladder or series of poly spots on one leg and then the other (muscular endurance).

Teachers, please note: This illustration is an example of the design you'll have to create for your students to use station 6. One way to create this design is to use tape on the gymnasium floor—if this is acceptable at your school.

TEACHING HINTS

- Use all of the sample station ideas in one lesson or use individual examples over a period of several lessons.
- Ask, "What daily activities use muscular strength and endurance?" Have students make a collage of pictures of people doing activities that require both muscular strength and endurance.

SAMPLE INCLUSION TIPS

Modifications will be specific to the station. For example:

- Station 1, Scooter Push-Away: A student in a wheelchair may give one push on the wheels with their arms to see how far their chair will travel.
- Station 5, Maimum Horizontal Jump: Have students with limited mobility step to the side and measure the distance of the step.
- Station 7, Mississippi Push-Ups: Allow students to substitute with wall push-ups or other modifications as needed.

ASSESSMENT

▓ Have students tell you an activity from one of the stations that use muscular strength (Scooter Push-Away, Maximum Vertical Jump, Maximum Horizontal Jump [Long Jump], Mississippi Push-Ups).

▓ Have students tell you an activity from one of the stations that uses muscular endurance (Scooter Travel, Repeating Step-Up, Power Jumps, Agility Hops).

4.2 Muscle Hustle

INTERMEDIATE LEVEL

Muscular strength involves the strongest force possible that a group of muscles can produce to perform a task. **Muscular endurance** is the ability to move your body or an object repeatedly without getting tired. For most activities, you use both muscular strength and endurance. If you do not use your muscles regularly, they can lose strength and endurance.

PURPOSE

Students will understand the definitions of muscular strength and muscular endurance by participating in several circuit activities that develop or demonstrate these components.

RELATIONSHIP TO NATIONAL STANDARDS

Physical Education Standard 4: The student achieves and maintains a health-enhancing level of physical fitness.

EQUIPMENT

■ Equipment needed for stations: basketballs, light volleyballs, four soccer balls, cones, lightweight medicine ball, bean bags, containers

■ Segmented music and player (optional)

PROCEDURE

1. Define muscular strength and endurance. Share or have students share a few examples of each. Explain that today students will participate in a circuit designed to build muscular strength and/or endurance, which in turn will enhance physical activity and motor performance. Describe the station activities to students.

Reproducibles

■ Muscle Hustle Station Signs (listing a sport, skill, or activity that requires muscular strength or endurance; see sidebar)

■ Muscle Hustle Score Sheet

STATION 1
Set or Bump

Perform a forearm pass (bump) or overhead pass (set) off the wall as many times as you can. How many did you complete? Does this skill require muscular strength, muscular endurance, or both?

Activity 4.2   Muscle Hustle Station Signs
From *Physical (best activity guide: Elementary level)*, 2nd edition, by NASPE, 2005, Champaign, IL: Human Kinetics

Name _____ Class _____ Date _____

Activity 4.2
Muscle Hustle Tracking Sheet

Station	Score (repetitions or time)	Muscular strength? (yes or no)	Muscular endurance? (yes or no)
Set or Bump			
Wall Lean Push-Ups			
Basketball Dribble			
Curl-Up Pass			
Soccer Score			
Wall Lean Chair Sits			
Target Pitches			
Push-Up, Pick Up			

Activity 4.2   Muscle Hustle Score Sheet
From *Physical (best activity guide: Elementary level)*, 2nd edition, by NASPE, 2005, Champaign, IL: Human Kinetics

2. Divide students into small groups and have each group go to a station, with a score sheet and a pencil for each student.

3. Signal students to perform the activity on the Muscle Hustle Sign at their station for 30 seconds, and record their total time or repetitions. Working individually or as a group, check off muscular strength and/or endurance.

4. Have students rotate from station to station.

5. Continue as long as desired.

© Human Kinetics

Muscle Hustle Sample Stations

Station 1—Set or Bump

Students perform a forearm pass (bump) or overhead pass (set) off a wall as many times as they can during their 30 seconds at the station. They count total bumps or sets.

Station 2—Wall-Lean Push-Ups

Students stand and lean into a wall with elbows straight but not locked. They perform as many wall-lean push-ups as they can during their 30 seconds at the station.

Station 3—Basketball Dribble

Students continually practice dribbling a basketball. They count how many successful dribbles they made during the 30 seconds at the station.

Station 4—Curl-Up Pass

Students lay in the curl-up position opposite a partner with one holding a lightweight medicine ball. Partners curl-up together, and on each curl-up pass the ball from one partner to the other. How many successful passes did they make in 30 seconds?

Station 5—Soccer Score

Using the inside of the foot, students try to "score" by hitting a cone or scoring a goal. They count the number of goals scored during the 30 seconds.

Station 6—Wall-Lean Chair Sits

Students sit in a chair position with their backs against the wall and hold the position as long as they can during their 30 seconds at the station.

Station 7—Target Pitches

Students pitch a ball as fast as possible yet under control at a target to score a hit. They count how many successful strikes they made into the target during their 30 seconds at the station.

Station 8—Push-Up, Pick Up

In a push-up position, students pick up beanbags and fill a container. They count how many beanbags they placed in the container during their 30 seconds at the station.

TEACHING HINTS

- Have students bring in pictures of athletes performing muscular strength and endurance activities in their sport/activity.
- Construct a bulletin board showing these pictures, and name the muscle groups being used.

SAMPLE INCLUSION TIPS

Station 1

- Change color of ball or use an auditory for student with visual impairment
- Change the size of the ball

Station 3

- Students can "air dribble" by tossing and catching the ball

Station 5

- Make the target larger or change the distance from the target
- Change object thrown to a beanbag or a yarn ball

ASSESSMENT

- Ask students to refer to their Muscle Hustle Score Sheet, and tell you for each activity whether they thought it used muscular strength, muscular endurance, or both, and why.
- Have students write short definitions of muscular strength and muscular endurance and give two examples of physical activities or sports that require muscular strength and endurance.
- Provide students with a list of physical activities and have them identify skills that require muscular strength and endurance. This example will give you a start:
  - **activity**—Baseball and softball
  - **muscular strength**—Throwing ball from center field
  - **muscular endurance**—Pitching for an inning

4.3 Talk to the Animals

PRIMARY LEVEL

Health benefits—Strong muscles allow us to participate in a variety of activities, including chores, work, and play. Muscles that have good endurance allow us to play and work safely for long periods. Among the many benefits to having good muscular strength and endurance are good posture, strong bones, and strong muscles.

PURPOSE

Students will identify several benefits related to muscular strength and endurance and learn how muscular strength and endurance play a role in developing strong, healthy bones.

RELATIONSHIP TO NATIONAL STANDARDS

Physical Education Standard 4: The student achieves and maintains a health-enhancing level of physical fitness. The student will support body weight momentarily by taking weight on the hands.

Health Education Standard 1: The student will comprehend concepts related to health promotion and disease prevention.

Health Education Standard 3: The student will demonstrate the ability to practice health-enhancing behaviors and reduce health risks.

EQUIPMENT

Music and player

PROCEDURE

1. Define muscular strength and endurance and discuss their benefits. Explain that today students will be performing animal walks to develop muscular strength and endurance. Review the Animal Walk Cards, making sure that students know what to do for each animal. Remind students to stay in their personal spaces while traveling about the activity area.

2. Spread the animal cards around the activity space.

3. Discuss the health benefits of muscular strength and endurance. (You may want to use an extra set of the reproducible pictures from the CD-ROM.)

4. Direct students to move to an animal card and start the music.

5. Ask students to act like the picture of the animal on the card.

Reproducible

- Animal Walk Cards (Copy and laminate as many sets as needed, depending on class size. There are seven examples on the CD-ROM.)

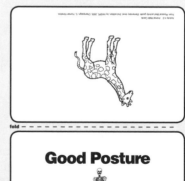

Good Posture

6. Stop the music and ask the students to turn the card over to discover a health benefit of muscular strength and endurance.

7. Ask a student to call out the benefit that they discovered. Ask what other students discovered the same benefit.

8. Start the music again, and have students move to another card in a locomotor pattern that you choose.

9. Repeat steps 4 through 6 until students have discussed several health benefits and have performed several animal walks.

TEACHING HINTS

© Human Kinetics

- In previewing the Animal Walk Cards before beginning the activity, spend an amount of time appropriate to the age and reading abilities of the students. Be sure to reinforce that the animal walks and other ways of traveling develop muscular strength and endurance as they learn about the benefits of these two parts of health-related fitness.

- As an extension to the activity, have students select one benefit that is important to them and develop a poster showing why that benefit is important.

SAMPLE INCLUSION TIP

Provide students with a list of animals prior to the class. The students can practice their interpretations for each animal.

ASSESSMENT

- Have students name two benefits of muscular strength and endurance that they learned in this activity.

- Have students tell the benefit written on the back of the Animal Walk Card that you are holding up.

4.4 Sport Roundup

INTERMEDIATE LEVEL

Health benefits—Strong muscles allow us to participate in a variety of activities, including chores, work, play, and sports. Muscles that have good endurance allow us to work or play safely for long periods. In addition to having the benefit of playing and working harder and longer, good muscular strength and endurance can have many other benefits, including stronger bones, a stronger heart, good posture, and injury prevention.

PURPOSE

- Students will understand the health benefits associated with muscular strength and endurance.
- Students will identify connections between specific activities and muscular fitness.
- Students will participate in physical activities that help develop muscular fitness through specific physical activities.

RELATIONSHIP TO NATIONAL STANDARDS

Physical Education Standard 4: The student achieves and maintains a health-enhancing level of physical fitness.

Health Education Standard 1: The student will comprehend concepts related to health promotion and disease prevention.

Health Education Standard 3: The student will demonstrate the ability to practice health-enhancing behaviors and reduce health risks.

Reproducibles

- Sport Roundup Station Signs
- Health Benefit Signs
- Sport Roundup Task Sheet

EQUIPMENT

- Energetic, upbeat music
- Clipboards and pencils (one per group)
- Jump ropes
- Low hurdles or small cones
- Ball, stick, puck, and so on, needed to practice goal scoring for any sport

Sample Station Ideas

1. Jump Rope Fun

Students jump rope, using multiple repetitions and sets to develop leg strength and endurance. Health benefit—stronger heart

2. Hurdler Leap

Students leap over a series of low obstacles on the ground, such as low hurdles or small cones, to improve leg strength. Health benefit—stronger bones

3. Score That Goal

Students take several shots on goal in a row (any sport). Health benefit—perform better

4. Kick Boxing

Students perform a variety of kicks and punches to develop upper body and lower body strength and endurance. Health benefit—stronger muscles

5. Strike Out

Students practice throwing form. Health benefit—prevents injury

6. Core Moves

From the pike position—clap hands together and then touch them to the floor repeatedly. From the pelvic raise position—alternately lift the right and left leg. Health benefit—good posture

7. Skating

Students pretend to skate in a pattern between and around cones, keeping the legs low to work the leg muscles. Health benefit—play and work longer

8. Line Dance

Have students perform a basic line dance routine, or other dance moves (such as those used in the activities You Should Be Dancing or Healthy Heart Hoe-Down from the aerobic fitness chapter). Health benefit—more energy

PROCEDURE

1. Using the eight Sport Round Up Station Signs or the Health Benefit Signs (provided on the CD-ROM), set up the stations around the activity space. Place the station activity and corresponding Health Benefit Signs side by side at each station. You may also create your own station signs for various sports and lifetime activities that interest your students.

2. Briefly review with the class, the definitions of muscular strength and muscular endurance. Also discuss the health benefits often associated with good muscular strength and endurance.

3. Divide students into small groups of four to six. Assign each group to a station.

4. Start music to signal students to perform the activity at that station. Stop the music to signal groups to stop and fill in their task sheet for that station. They should write in the health benefit that corresponds with the activity and a brief explanation of how the activity relates to the health benefit (for example, jumping rope works the leg muscles but also increases the heart rate, working the heart and making it stronger).

5. Start music again to signal students to proceed to the next station, and continue through the stations or until you have reached a predetermined time.

6. Discuss the task sheets as a group.

© Human Kinetics

TEACHING HINTS

▧ Make sure the activity stations are equal in time. Use a stopwatch or segmented or interval music to ensure consistent timing.

▧ To promote critical thinking, as a variation for older students, scatter the health benefit signs in the center of the activity space, and after performing the station, have students look through the health benefits and select one that matches their activity, and fill that in along with the explanation of their choice on their task card.

SAMPLE INCLUSION TIPS

Modifications to each activity:

▧ Jump rope—jumping over lines, secured hula hoop, or rope

▧ Hurdle—change the height of the hurdle

▧ Scoring—change the size of the puck, use a handled hockey stick, add color to the goal

▧ Kick boxing—have students perform a sitting curl-up in a wheelchair, add weight if needed by using a medicine ball

▧ Strike out—change the size and weight of the ball, use yarn ball or bean bags

▧ Skating—student in wheelchair can move in a pattern between and around cones.

When changing stations, use visual cues, such as red and green flags, for students with hearing impairments.

ASSESSMENT

▧ Collect task sheets after first asking students to identify which health benefit(s) are most important to them, and to write an answer on their task sheets.

▧ Have groups create their own station to improve muscular strength and endurance, and explain why they chose that activity, how it relates to muscular strength and endurance of that particular sport/activity, and what health benefits may be associated with that activity.

4.5 Muscular Strength and Endurance Activity Picture Chart

PRIMARY LEVEL

Frequency is how many days per week you perform muscular strength and endurance activities. You should participate in strength and endurance activities two to three times a week. Daily chores and tasks require muscular strength and endurance.

PURPOSE

Students will understand and demonstrate how many days each week they should perform strength and endurance activities.

RELATIONSHIP TO NATIONAL STANDARDS

Physical Education Standard 3: The student participates regularly in physical activity.

Health Education Standard 3: The student will demonstrate the ability to practice health-enhancing behaviors and reduce health risks.

EQUIPMENT

Everyday items for stations suggested in "Teaching Hints" section.

PROCEDURE

1. Review the definitions and explanations of muscular strength and muscular endurance.

2. Define frequency (how often) and discuss the importance of regularly performing activities that require muscular strength and muscular endurance.

3. Encourage students to offer muscular activity examples from outside the physical education class (for example, carrying groceries into the house will build both muscular strength and endurance, sweeping the floor will build muscular endurance in arm muscles, riding a bike will build muscular endurance of the legs).

4. Encourage students to find different ways to stay active. Give them examples that fit within their community (using a public pool, visiting a local park, biking with family members and friends).

5. Pass out the Muscular Strength and Endurance Activity Picture Chart and ask students to work with their parents at home to fill it out for the next week.

Reproducible

■ Muscular Strength and Endurance Activity Picture Chart, one per student

Name: _____ Class: _____ Date: _____

Activity 4.5
Muscular Strength and Endurance
Activity Picture Chart

Circle the activities that you have done in the past week or in a blank space draw an activity that you have done. How many days did you do this activity? If it is more than one, write that number by the picture.

Activity 4.5 Muscular Strength and Endurance Activity Picture Chart
From *Physical Best activity guide: Elementary level, 2nd edition*, by NASPE, 2005, Champaign, IL: Human Kinetics.

TEACHING HINTS

- Encourage students to find different ways to stay active. Give them examples that fit within their community.
- Create stations at which students use everyday items at stations to show how they can get a workout using items in their homes (for example, lifting milk jugs into the refrigerator, sweeping dried rice or pasta into a dustpan, climbing steps or climbing one step repeatedly to simulate a staircase).
- Construct a bulletin board with hand-drawn or magazine pictures of the different activities that the students found to do.
- Have a family day in physical education when family members join students in activities that the family can do at home to keep in shape.

© Human Kinetics

SAMPLE INCLUSION TIPS

- Discuss with each student what activities they participate in outside of school.
- Use this activity as an opportunity for diversity training. Have students with disabilities share or demonstrate the activities they participate in outside of school.

ASSESSMENT

- Have students tell you how many days per week they perform muscular strength and endurance activities.
- Collect the homework sheet and lead a class discussion on the activities circled and added.
- Have students discuss with the class their favorite muscular strength or muscular endurance activity.

4.6

Muscular Strength and Endurance Activity Log

INTERMEDIATE LEVEL

Frequency describes how often you perform the targeted health-related physical activity. For muscular strength and endurance activity sessions, frequency should be two to three times per week, although daily activities such as carrying groceries, a backpack, or raking leaves also develop muscular strength and endurance.

PURPOSE

Students will understand and demonstrate how many days per week they should perform muscular strength and endurance activities.

RELATIONSHIP TO NATIONAL STANDARDS

Physical Education Standard 3: The student participates regularly in physical activity.

Health Education Standard 3: The student will demonstrate the ability to practice health-enhancing behaviors and reduce health risks.

EQUIPMENT

Everyday items for stations suggested in "Teaching Hints" section.

PROCEDURE

1. Review or define frequency. Have the students brainstorm some ways that they perform muscular strength and endurance activities in their everyday lives (for example, carrying groceries into the house will build both muscular strength and endurance, raking leaves will build muscular endurance in arm muscles, and riding a bike will build muscular endurance of the legs). Encourage them to use physical activity examples from outside physical education class. (See also Sport Roundup examples, beginning on page 73.)

2. Pass out the Muscular Strength and Endurance Activity Log and ask students to work with their parents at home to fill it out for the next one to two weeks.

Reproducible

■ Muscular Strength and Endurance Activity Log

TEACHING HINTS

- Use class time effectively by having the brainstorm discussion during a cool-down or stretch.

- Create stations using everyday items to show how the students can get a workout using items in their homes (for example, lifting canned foods onto a shelf, sweeping dried rice or pasta into a dustpan, climbing steps or climbing one step repeatedly to simulate a staircase).

- Construct a bulletin board with student drawings or magazine pictures of the different activities that the students found to do.

- Have a family day in physical education when family members join students in activities that the family can do at home to keep in shape.

SAMPLE INCLUSION TIP

Provide parents and students with a list of agencies (departments of parks and recreation or therapeutic recreation programs) that offer a variety of programs for students with disabilities outside of the school environment.

ASSESSMENT

- Have students tell or write a definition of frequency and compare their log to the number of days per week they should participate in muscular strength and endurance activities.

- Collect the homework sheet and lead a class discussion on activities that the students participate in most frequently.

4.7

Statue, Statue

PRIMARY LEVEL

Intensity is how hard you work your muscles during an activity.

PURPOSE

Students will cooperate in pairs to create shapes to develop their muscular strength and endurance. Students will explore the concept of intensity as it relates to the activity.

RELATIONSHIP TO NATIONAL STANDARDS

Physical Education Standard 4: The student will achieve and maintain a health-enhancing level of physical fitness.

Physical Education Standard 5: The student exhibits responsible personal and social behavior that respects self and others in physical activity settings.

EQUIPMENT

Poly spots or cones

PROCEDURE

1. Using a picture of the body with muscle groups identified (such as the one provided on the CD-ROM), introduce the names of major muscle groups in the upper body (for example: shoulders—deltoids, chest—pectoralis, and so on) and the lower body (for example: thighs—quadriceps, buttocks—gluteals).

2. Explain the concept of intensity as it relates to muscular strength and endurance, and explain that they will be participating in an activity that will require varying intensities, depending on the shapes that they create.

3. Divide students into pairs or small groups of two or three students each, and direct them to find a spot in the general space. You may use cones or poly spots scattered around the floor, and have them move to one spot.

4. Direct each group to create a statue shape together that focuses on the upper body, lower body, or a combination of upper and lower body muscles. They must then hold the shape for several seconds. They can do so while counting "Statue, statue…" for the number of seconds you select.

5. Signal students to release the shape, and wiggle or shake it out. Then they create the same shape again, and hold it several seconds, and finally a third time—(totaling three repetitions to make one set).

6. Repeat steps 3 and 4, having students focus on another set of muscle groups (lower body, if upper body was first used, for example).

Reproducible

■ Muscle Groups Picture

Shoulder-deltoids

Arms - biceps

Torso - abdominals

Legs - quadriceps

Chest - pectorals

Activity 4.7   Muscle Groups Picture
From *Physical best activity guide: Elementary level*, 2nd edition, by NASPE, 2005, Champaign, IL: Human Kinetics.

TEACHING HINTS

- Stress safety. For example, walk around and monitor students, ensuring that they are not performing unsafe moves such as inverted balances. Do not allow horseplay.
- Select poses and have two students demonstrate each pose if necessary, before scattering pairs.
- Practice favorite shapes in future classes and then have groups create a Statue, Statue Park as part of a parent night demonstration. Upon the command "Statue, Statue," pairs perform a new pose of their or your choosing. Explain to parents the concept of intensity and how they can help their children develop muscular strength and endurance at home (see Muscular Strength and Endurance Newsletter).

SAMPLE INCLUSION TIP

Students that have only upper body mobility should make shapes using their upper body.

ASSESSMENT

- Circulate during the activity, asking groups to explain the concept of intensity to you. Have (or help) them point out what muscles feel the highest intensity. (Shapes that emphasize larger muscle groups are likely to feel higher intensity than shapes that focus on smaller muscle groups.)
- Have pairs demonstrate the shape they believe caused the highest intensity.

4.8 Move and Improve Obstacle Course

INTERMEDIATE LEVEL

Intensity is how hard you work your muscles during an activity.

PURPOSE

Students will cooperate in small groups to navigate and modify an obstacle course to develop their muscular strength and endurance while learning about and applying the concept of intensity related to the FITT Guidelines.

RELATIONSHIP TO NATIONAL STANDARDS

Physical Education Standard 4: The student will achieve and maintain a health-enhancing level of physical fitness.

Physical Education Standard 5: The student exhibits responsible personal and social behavior that respects self and others in physical activity settings.

EQUIPMENT

See sample stations and equipment needed for each in sidebar.

Reproducible

None

PROCEDURE

1. Set up an obstacle course that contains activities focusing on muscular strength and endurance. Sample course stations are included in the sidebar. Use these or create your own.

2. Review the FITT Guidelines, explaining that this activity will focus on Intensity (how hard). Also explain that the FITT Guidelines are personal, and should be based on their current, individual fitness level.

3. Review the obstacle course, perhaps asking one or more students to demonstrate at each station.

4. Discuss safety when navigating obstacle courses. Use staggered starts, controlled movements and so on. To allow for students moving at varying paces, set up multiple sets of equipment for those stations which require that to accommodate more than one student, or signal station changes.

5. Have students complete the course. When the class has gone through the course, divide students into groups and assign each group to one station of the course.

© Human Kinetics

6. Ask the groups to work together to create a variation on the station's activity to increase its intensity. Give them time to work on the changes and circulate the room to check for safety. (Examples: Hold each curl-up in the up position for 3 seconds, log roll once to the right then roll left—taking out momentum and adding more muscular control.)

7. Have each group demonstrate their variation.

Sample Obstacle Course Stations

Animal Walk

Description
Perform animal walks such as a dog, crab, inchworm, and so on, in and around a series of cones (such as four cones set up in a square).

Equipment
Cones

Do the Hoop/Jump the Ladder

Description
Jump, leap, or hop through an agility ladder or series of hoops.

Equipment
Agility ladder or hoops

Curl-Ups

Description
Lie down and perform 10 curl-ups.

Equipment
Mat and curl-up strip

Commando Crawl

Description
Belly crawl down the length of several mats or through a tunnel.

Equipment
Mats or tunnel

Step Box Shuffle

Description
Step up and down sideways across several steps lined up in a row, then step back to the starting point.

Equipment
Step benches

Push-Up Strike Down

Description
In a regular or modified push-up position, strike down pins with a ball.

Equipment
Ball and bowling pins or similar objects

Scooter Push/Pull

Description
Sit on scooter and pull with legs and push with arms around a series of cones (such as four cones set up in a square).

Equipment
Scooter and cones

Poly Spot Leap

Description
Leap over a series of poly spots, landing between the spots, then turn around and leap back.

Equipment
Poly spots

Log Roll

Description
Holding a ball with both hands overhead and lying down on a mat, roll the length of the mat, then roll back.

Equipment
Mat and ball

Jump Box

Description
Jump up onto a box and step down (5-10 times).

Equipment
Step bench

TEACHING HINTS

- Set up obstacle courses before class or, when revisiting the activity, have students set them up.
- For safety reasons, be sure to monitor modifications of obstacle courses. Depending on the maturity and knowledge level of the students, you may be able to have them discuss, modify, and navigate their stations simultaneously, or you may need to signal each station and control the action more closely.
- Incorporate skills practice by setting up obstacles that include elements, such as running while dribbling a basketball or soccer ball in and out of cones. Another obstacle could have the students pretending to swing a bat or racket for a number

of reps (if you use real bats or rackets, ensure that students have enough space to swing safely and understand how to maintain personal space).

■ Practice favorite courses in future classes, factoring in the time concept of FITT. For example, the longer the obstacle course takes, the greater the fitness benefit, all other factors being equal.

■ Alternatively, revisit the favorite courses and focus on the type, or specificity, concept of FITT. For example, identify which parts of a course develop upper body strength and endurance, which develop abdominal strength and endurance, and which develop lower body strength and endurance.

SAMPLE INCLUSION TIP

Modify the obstacle course stations to meet the needs of individual students. For example, use light weights or resistance bands in place of push-ups, and seated leg extensions in place of jumping.

ASSESSMENT

■ Leave enough time to have each group share one or two changes they made and how those modifications increased or decreased intensity.

■ For homework, have individual students write a few sentences describing their group's most intense obstacle course (or the one that was individually the most intense for him or her). As an alternative, have the entire class complete the Sample Inclusion Tip described earlier.

4.9

Time Flies!

INTERMEDIATE LEVEL

Time is how long an activity takes. In the case of muscular strength and endurance, time may be the time the sets and reps take plus the rest between the sets.

PURPOSE

- Students will participate in a muscular strength and endurance workout while reviewing or learning the definitions of repetition, set, and workout.
- Students will learn about the concept of time as it relates to muscular strength and endurance, that is, that time involves doing the reps and sets as well as resting between sets.

RELATIONSHIP TO NATIONAL STANDARDS

Physical Education Standard 4: The student achieves and maintains a health-enhancing level of physical fitness.

EQUIPMENT

- Stopwatches
- Stretch bands
- Step benches
- Lightweight dumbbells

Reproducibles

- Time Flies! Rep and Set Poster (optional)
- Time Flies! Station Signs
- Time Flies! Worksheet (one per two students)

Time Flies! Rep and Set

One repetition—Doing an activity or exercise once. We often just say, "Rep" for short.

One set—Several repetitions (reps) of the same activity or exercise.

A workout—One or more sets of reps. Each set may be of the same exercise or a combination of different exercises.

TIME—How long you do an activity. In the case of muscular strength and endurance, time may be more specifically the time the sets and reps take plus the rest between sets. For example, two sets of eight reps might take the following amount of time:

8 reps (20 seconds) + 15 seconds rest +
8 reps (20 seconds) = 55 seconds total **TIME**

Activity 4.9 Time Flies! Rep and Set Poster
From Physical Best activity guide: Elementary level, 2nd edition, by NASPE, 2005, Champaign, IL: Human Kinetics.

Squats

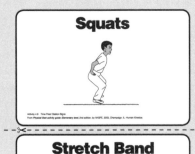

Activity 4.9 Time Flies! Station Signs
From Physical Best activity guide: Elementary level, 2nd edition, by NASPE, 2005, Champaign, IL: Human Kinetics.

Stretch Band Chest Press

Activity 4.9 Time Flies! Station Signs
From Physical Best activity guide: Elementary level, 2nd edition, by NASPE, 2005, Champaign, IL: Human Kinetics.

Name: _____ Class: _____ Date: _____

Activity 4.9
Time Flies! Worksheet

Name of activity	Time
1.	
2.	
3.	
4.	
5.	
6.	
7.	
8.	
9.	
10.	
Total Time	

Activity 4.9 Time Flies! Worksheet
From Physical Best activity guide: Elementary level, 2nd edition, by NASPE, 2005, Champaign, IL: Human Kinetics.

PROCEDURE

1. Set up muscular strength and endurance activity stations around the room. Use the Time Flies! Station Signs provided with the CD-ROM reproducibles, or create your own. Fill out the activities that you will use on the Time Flies! Worksheet, and make enough copies to have one for every two students.

2. Define repetition, set, and time as they relate to muscular strength and endurance activities. For a visual, use the Time Flies! Rep and Set Poster on the CD-ROM.

3. Divide students into pairs. Give each pair one Time Flies! Worksheet and a stopwatch.

4. Review and demonstrate the muscular strength and endurance activities listed on the Time Flies! Worksheets.

5. Assign each pair a station, distributing pairs equally among the stations. Explain that for each station, pairs should take turns performing one set of 10 repetitions, with each student completing two sets of 10 repetitions before moving on to the next station. They should start the stopwatch before the first student performs the first set, and stop it after the second student performs the second set, resetting the stopwatch between stations.

6. At the conclusion of the activity, students add all times together to find the total length of their workout. Explain that in addition to the time it took each of them to perform their repetitions and sets, the time their partner was active, and the time it took them to rotate stations (their rest time) also factor into their total workout time.

TEACHING HINTS

■ Be sure to have students warm up and cool down properly before and after this activity.

■ If needed, before beginning the activity, talk the entire class through one station not on the worksheet, with both partners performing both sets and running the stopwatch.

- If students first need to build more muscular strength and endurance, be especially careful to tailor your use of the worksheet. For example, have students do fewer sets and fewer reps and allow more time between sets until students are in better condition.

- Individualize the workout further by allowing students to choose and record their own number of reps per set.

SAMPLE INCLUSION TIP

Always be alert to each student's ability to perform body weight exercises. Then modify as needed to increase success and safety. For example, allowing students to place one or both knees on the floor can modify activities such as push-ups. Curl-up variations include lying on the back with knees bent and lifting the head or sitting and then slowly lowering the body backward.

ASSESSMENT

- Ask the class to write or tell a definition of a "workout." (Repetitions and sets, rest time can also be included for bonus points!)

- Ask the class to describe how they can change the time it takes to complete a workout. (Number of repetitions, sets, amount of rest time, pace of the activities)

4.10 Muscle Trek

PRIMARY LEVEL

Specificity refers to the kind of activity that you do. When working on muscles, the muscles that you exercise are specific to the activity.

PURPOSE

Through a group exploration activity, students will learn that specific exercises train specific muscle groups.

RELATIONSHIP TO NATIONAL STANDARDS

Physical Education Standard 4: The student achieves and maintains a health-enhancing level of physical fitness.

EQUIPMENT

- Needed according to the activities you select
- Music with a space theme and player

PROCEDURE

1. Prepare 5 to 10 activities for the body's major muscle groups, using a planetary theme. Each planet should be named a major body part. Use the Muscle Trek Planet Signs provided in the reproducible, or create your own.

2. Tell students that you will be taking a muscle trek together, visiting various planets on your star ships and stopping to experience each planet's muscle group.

3. Have students spread and on your cue move in general space to the music while pretending to pilot their star ship. Continue for 20 to 30 seconds.

4. Signal students to stop and land their ship. Hold up a planet card in front of them and tell them the planet name, using the appropriate anatomical name of the muscle as the planet name. Then explain what body part you mean by using the general body part name. (For example: Stop and land your ship. We have reached Planet Deltoid. The deltoid muscles are part of your shoulders.)

5. Have students participate with you in one set of approximately 10 repetitions of an activity that works that muscle group.

6. Signal students to return to their ships and move through space again, and repeat until cards have been completed.

Reproducible

- Muscle Trek Planet Signs

Planet Pectorals (chest)

Activity 4.10 Muscle Trek Planet Signs
From *Physical Best activity guide: Elementary level*, 2nd edition, by NASPE, 2005, Champaign, IL: Human Kinetics.

TEACHING HINTS

- Be sure that your students are warmed-up properly to participate in the activity.

- Select muscular activities that require little or no equipment. If equipment is needed, place it around the perimeter of the activity space and have students pick it up when you stop at that planet, and drop it off before resuming their movement in space.

- This activity can easily be adapted to teach specificity for flexibility by switching stretches for the muscular activities.

SAMPLE INCLUSION TIP

Students should be able to move at their own pace before landing their ship. Allow students more time to complete repetitions, or allow them to complete fewer repetitions as necessary.

ASSESSMENT

Hold up the planet cards and again name the anatomical and general body part terms. Ask students if they remember the muscular activity that corresponded with that planet. Help if needed. Then explain to students that the activity worked that body part specifically, and therefore those were the muscles that benefited from the activity.

4.11 Shuffle and Hustle

INTERMEDIATE LEVEL

Specificity, or **type,** refers to the kind of physical activity that you do. In muscular strength and endurance activities, the muscles "worked" are specific to the exercises performed.

PURPOSE

- Students will be able to define specificity (type) with respect to muscular strength and endurance.
- Students will be able to list exercises or activities that develop specific muscle groups.

RELATIONSHIP TO NATIONAL STANDARDS

Physical Education Standard 4: The student achieves and maintains a health-enhancing level of physical fitness.

EQUIPMENT

- A deck of cards
- Upbeat music and player (optional)

Any equipment needed for the exercises at each station. If using those provided on the CD-ROM, you will need:

- Lightweight dumbbells
- Stretch bands
- Step benches
- Mats

PROCEDURE

1. Place a poster with a different playing card suit symbol and list of exercises for specific muscle groups on each of the four walls of the activity area to create four stations. If conducting the activity outdoors, use slotted cones or another means to secure the posters. Use the posters provided on the CD-ROM reproducibles, or create your own.

2. As a group, practice the exercises that coincide with each of the four muscle groupings selected. While doing this, introduce students to the anatomical names for the muscle groups, and focus on teaching proper form for executing the exercises. Also, explain that different exercises work different muscles (concept of specificity).

Reproducible

- Shuffle and Hustle Suit Posters

♥ **Squats**
♥ **Wall sits**
♥ **Step-ups**
♥ **Calf raises**

Activity 4.11 Shuffle and Hustle Suit Posters
From *Physical Best activity guide: Elementary level,* 2nd edition, by NASPE, 2005, Champaign, IL, Human Kinetics.

3. Break the class into small groups of two or three students.

4. Place a deck of cards with face cards removed, in the center of the activity space. Have each group draw a card from the deck and go to the poster that has that suit.

5. They then choose a specific exercise from that suit's designated muscle groups, and perform the number of repetitions that correspond with the number on their card.

6. Students come back and place their card in a bucket, and draw a new card from the remaining stack. They continue until all cards have been used, at which point the cards can be reshuffled for a second round, and continue until you've reached a designated time or number of rounds.

TEACHING HINTS

- Look for extra large playing cards to use—they will be easier to handle and keep together.
- Throughout the activity, circulate the room to provide assistance and feedback with the exercises.

SAMPLE INCLUSION TIP

Assign a peer assistant to a child with a visual impairment to help the child travel safely to and from the walls as well as to read the number of the shuffled card and perform the activity.

ASSESSMENT

Point to a muscle group on your body and ask students to name an exercise that they did during the activity that worked those muscles. As an alternative or in addition—ask them to name the muscle(s) as well.

4.12 Push-Up Curl-Up Challenge

INTERMEDIATE LEVEL

Progression refers to how an individual should increase overload. Proper progression involves a gradual increase in the level of exercise manipulated by increasing frequency, intensity, or time, or a combination of all three components.

PURPOSE

Students will practice the concept and skill of applying progression as it relates to muscular strength and endurance.

RELATIONSHIP TO NATIONAL STANDARDS

Physical Education Standard 3: The student participates regularly in physical activity.

Physical Education Standard 4: The student achieves and maintains a health-enhancing level of physical fitness.

Health Education Standard 3: The student will demonstrate the ability to practice health-enhancing behaviors and reduce health risks.

Health Education Standard 6: The student will demonstrate the ability to use goal-setting and decision-making skills to enhance health.

Reproducibles

- Push-Up Challenge Poster
- Curl-Up Challenge Poster
- Push-Up Curl-Up Challenge Log

Push-Up Challenges

Push-Up Challenge list is written in a general progression of increasing intensity.

- Wall push-ups
- "Mississippi" count push-up
- Hands back and forth over a line
- Sailor salutes
- Pass object back and forth between hands
- Wave hello, switching hands
- Alternately raise feet
- Stack the beanbags (or rocks) in a bucket
- Inchworm push-up (walk hands out and in)
- Balance object on your back push-up
- Narrow hands push-up
- Wide hands push-up
- 4-count push-up (2 down, 2 up)
- Wide leg push-up
- One foot on top of the other push-up

Activity 4.12 Push-Up Challenge Poster
From *Physical Best activity guide: Elementary level*, 2nd edition, by NASPE, 2005, Champaign, IL: Human Kinetics.

Curl-Up Challenges

Individual Curl-Ups:
- 4-count curl-up (knees, toes, knees, floor)
- Angled curl-ups (alternating toward the right knee, and left knee)
- Reverse curl-up
- Legs in air curl-up
- Chant curl-up (1, 2, 3, 4—strength is what we're looking for!) going up, then repeat going down

Partner Curl-Ups—facing each other:
- High fives
- Shake hands
- Pass the object

Activity 4.12 Curl-Up Challenge Poster
From *Physical Best activity guide: Elementary level*, 2nd edition, by NASPE, 2005, Champaign, IL: Human Kinetics.

Name: _____ Class: _____ Date: _____

Name of push-up challenge selected: _____

Name of curl-up challenge selected: _____

Activity 4.12
Push-Up Curl-Up Challenge Log

Week 1	Push-up total count (3 sets)	Curl-up total count (3 sets)
Day 1		
Day 2		
Day 3		
Week 2		
Day 1		
Day 2		
Day 3		

Initial push-up result: _____ Final push-up result: _____

Initial curl-up result: _____ Final curl-up result: _____

Activity 4.12 Push-Up Curl-Up Challenge Log
From *Physical Best activity guide: Elementary level*, 2nd edition, by NASPE, 2005, Champaign, IL: Human Kinetics.

EQUIPMENT

Curl-Up Challenge equipment

- ■ Curl-up strips
- ■ Mats
- ■ Balls

Push-Up Challenge equipment

- ■ Balls
- ■ Beanbags
- ■ Buckets

PROCEDURE

1. Describe progression as it relates to frequency, intensity, time, and type. Teach and allow students to practice push-up and curl-up positions to ensure correct technique. Remind students that each individual must work from his or her current ability to gradually progress and achieve better performance. Remind students that they are each improving as individuals, not competing with one another.

2. Then have them write down in their Push-Up Curl-Up Challenge Log (see reproducible) how many push-ups and curl-ups they currently can perform according to the *FITNESSGRAM* protocols. You may also help them select a reasonable goal that they would like to achieve on their follow-up test. If they have not recently performed the assessments, conduct them as a class, and have them record the numbers on their log.

3. Introduce students to the activities on the Push-Up Challenge and Curl-Up Challenge Posters.

4. Direct each student to work in a personal space. Have each student choose one push-up challenge from the poster, and, beginning slowly, perform the exercise for a predetermined time, or for a range of repetitions. Students rest and then repeat the same exercise challenge for a second set and then a third set (depending on individual ability). Students should record their results on the log—writing the challenge selected and the total number of repetitions completed.

5. Repeat step 3, this time having students choose one curl-up challenge.

6. Bring students together as a group and assign them an out-of-class challenge. They should perform their push-up and curl-up challenges for three nonconsecutive days per week over the next two weeks, and record the results on their log (their first day of week one will have been completed in class). They should aim to meet or exceed the total repetitions completed in class.

7. At the conclusion of the two weeks, have students bring in completed logs to class, and repeat the *FITNESSGRAM* push-up and curl-up assessments, and write the results on the log.

TEACHING HINTS

▧ Review the concept of a "workout": repetitions + sets = workout

▧ If class is held at least three times per week, the challenges and logging can be done in class.

▧ Ask the school's after-school care providers to provide for space, time, and other support for students to work on their logs.

▧ To further reinforce the concept of progression, repeat the activity periodically throughout the school year and compare logs.

SAMPLE INCLUSION TIPS

To modify push-ups:

▧ Use weights, while maintaining flexed arms and muscle contractions

▧ Pick up weighted object tied to a rope

▧ Wrist curls—hold a rod with a rope attached to a weight and have student wrap string around rod using only wrist movements.

▧ Wall push-up

To modify curl-ups:

▧ Perform a seated curl-up using weight if needed, can also move side to side

▧ Have partner hold students' feet

▧ Perform a curl-up with arms placed at your side and touch the back of your heels

ASSESSMENT

▧ Collect the Push-Up Curl-Up Challenge Logs to evaluate the number of times the challenges were practiced.

▧ Ask students to describe what progression means in terms of health-related fitness, and the FITT Guidelines.

▧ Discuss with the class reasons they may have progressed. For example, maybe they were doing activities that helped them progress in the assessments. Also discuss why they may not have progressed. For example, some days you feel better and stronger than other days and they may have had a better day at the start of the challenge; progression can take more time; or perhaps they did not choose a challenge that provided enough overload to progress.

4.13 Muscular Strength and Endurance FITT Log

INTERMEDIATE LEVEL

Progression refers to how an individual should increase **overload**. Proper progression involves a gradual increase in the level of exercise that is manipulated by increasing frequency, intensity, or time, or a combination of all three components.

PURPOSE

- Students will learn and apply the training principles of progression and overload.
- Students will learn and apply the training principles of progression and overload for muscular strength and endurance, by completing a FITT log and worksheet.

RELATIONSHIP TO NATIONAL STANDARDS

Physical Education Standard 3: The student participates regularly in physical activity.

Physical Education Standard 4: The student will achieve and maintain a health-enhancing level of physical fitness.

Health Education Standard 3: The student will demonstrate the ability to practice health-enhancing behaviors and reduce health risks.

EQUIPMENT

Pencil for each student

PROCEDURE

1. Briefly, review the two-word definitions of the aspects of FITT—frequency (how often), intensity (how hard), time (how long), and type (what kind).

Reproducibles

- Muscular Strength and Endurance FITT Log
- Muscular Strength and Endurance FITT Log Worksheet

2. Ask students to offer brief examples of how they applied the FITT Guidelines to muscular strength and endurance in previous health-related fitness activities.

3. Share descriptions of the concepts of progression and overload.

4. Distribute one blank Muscular Strength and Endurance FITT Log to each student. Review each category and how it relates to each aspect of FITT.

5. Ask class to share muscular activities they enjoy and tell them to choose one and write it in their log.

6. Have the students write their name on the log.

7. Assign students to log their muscular strength and endurance physical activity performed outside class one week.

8. Have students complete week 1 of the FITT Log.

9. Guide students in setting goals for progression and overload and write them on the Muscular Strength and Endurance FITT Log Worksheet.

10. At the end of each week, meet with the class to discuss their progress and set new goals.

TEACHING HINTS

- Ask students at each class meeting how their logs are coming along.
- Require parent or guardian initials if necessary to encourage participation.
- Have students demonstrate the home-based activity ideas at an open house.
- Ask the school's after-school care providers to provide space, time, and other support for students to add to their logs.
- Tie in the *FITNESSGRAM* muscular strength and endurance assessments with this activity.

SAMPLE INCLUSION TIP

Help students with special circumstances come up with alternative activities to suit their needs and abilities. You can modify activities suggested earlier in this chapter, provide suggestions for students who must stay indoors because of safety or space constraints, or otherwise help students develop activity ideas that will work for them.

ASSESSMENT

After the month, have students review their logs with you and write about their experience by answering questions such as the following:

- Were you able to safely build up to a higher level of intensity over the course of the month, do the activities more frequently each week, or spend more time doing each activity? Which changes did you make, if any?

■ If you were able to make changes, how might the changes have affected your muscular fitness?

■ If you did not make changes, what might you be able to do differently in the future?

Realize that many factors, such as the child's initial level of fitness and participation (if already high, they may not progress for that reason), and other personal factors may affect the answers to these questions. Keeping this in mind, focus on the assessment as a means to teach and reinforce the concepts of progression and overload.

CHAPTER

5

Flexibility

Chapter Contents

- Defining Flexibility
- Teaching Guidelines for Flexibility
- Training Methods for Flexibility
- Motor Skill Development Through Flexibility Activities
- Flexibility Newsletter
- Activities

Flexibility is the ability to move a joint through its complete range of motion (ACSM 2000). Children can get an idea of how flexible they are by answering the question, "How well do you bend, stretch, and twist?" Our goal is to develop and maintain normal joint range of motion. Keep in mind that having too much mobility predisposes people to injury and is just as bad as having too little.

Being flexible can bring about many benefits:

▓ Decreased muscle tension and increased relaxation (I can sleep better)

▓ Greater ease of movement (I can move easier)

▓ Improved coordination (I can perform better in sport or dance)

▓ Increased range of motion (I can bend, stretch, and twist into many positions)

▓ Reduced risk of injury (I can move safely)

▓ Better body awareness and postural alignment (I can stand tall)

▓ Improved circulation and air exchange (I can breathe easier)

▓ Smoother and easier contractions (My muscles work better)

▓ Decreased muscle soreness (I am less sore after playing hard)

▓ Possible prevention of low back pain and other spinal problems (I can sit at my desk all morning without my back feeling sore)

▓ Improved personal appearance and self-image (I feel good about myself)

▓ Facilitates the development and maintenance of motor skills (I can do a variety of activities)

Defining Flexibility

There are two types of flexibility (static and dynamic) with four types of stretches (static, active, PNF, and passive) that foster the development of flexibility and improved range of motion.

▓ **Static flexibility** is the amount of motion at a joint and is limited by the person's tolerance to the stretch.

▓ **Dynamic (ballistic) flexibility** is the rate of increase in tension in a relaxed muscle as the person stretches it (Knudson, Magnusson, and McHugh 2000).

▓ A **static stretch** is a slow, sustained stretch of the muscle, held for 10 to 30 seconds at the point of mild discomfort, and backed off slightly (or held just before reaching the point of discomfort).

▓ In an **active stretch,** the participant provides the force of the stretch (for example, in the sit-and-reach, the person leans forward and reaches as far as possible).

▓ In a **passive stretch,** a partner provides the force of the stretch (see figure 7.3 in *Physical Education for Lifelong Fitness: The Physical Best Teacher's Guide, Second Edition*).

▓ **Proprioceptive neuromuscular facilitation (PNF)** is a static stretch using combinations of the active and passive stretching techniques.

At the elementary level, the focus is on active static stretching, not dynamic (ballistic) stretching. At this level, children are not ready to work with partners to improve flexibility or to perform PNF exercises.

Teaching Guidelines for Flexibility

As in all areas of health-related fitness, the principles of training (progression, overload, specificity, regularity, and individuality) must be applied when teaching flexibility concepts to students. The FITT Guidelines (table 5.1) also play a key role in improving flexibility. In applying the principles of training and the FITT Guidelines, be aware of the factors that affect flexibility (see *Physical Education for Lifelong Fitness: The Physical Best Teacher's Guide*, Second Edition) and therefore the improvement that you may or may not observe.

● ●

TABLE 5.1 FITT Guidelines Applied to Flexibility

Frequency	Three times per week, preferably daily and after a warm-up to raise muscle temperature.
Intensity	Slow elongation of the muscle to the point of mild discomfort and back off slightly.
Time	Up to 4-5 stretches per muscle or muscle group. Hold each stretch 10-30 sec. Always warm-up properly prior to stretching.
Type	The preferred stretch for the classroom is slow static stretching for all muscles or muscle groups.

NOTE: Although 10-30 sec is recommended as the length of time to hold a stretch, an advanced student may hold a stretch up to 60 sec.

Modified from Knudson, D.V., P. Magnusson, and M. McHugh. 2000. Current issues in flexibility fitness. In C. Corbin and B. Pangrazi, eds., *The president's council on physical fitness and sports digest*, 3rd ser., no. 10, Washington, DC: Department of Health and Human Services.

Modified from American College of Sports Medicine (ACSM). 2001. *ACSM's Resource Manual for Guidelines for Exercise Testing and Prescription*. 4th ed. Philadelphia: Lippincott, Williams, and Wilkins.

Factors That Affect Flexibility

- Failure to adhere to a regular program
- Muscle temperature
- Age and gender (Knudson, Magnusson, and McHugh 2000)
- Tissue interference (Heyward 2002)
- Muscle tension
- Poor coordination and strength during active movement
- Pain
- Lack of proper warm-up (Alter 1998; Knudson, Magnusson, and McHugh 2000)
- Certain diseases (Blanchard 1999)

Training Methods for Flexibility

Choose a variety of flexibility exercises and a variety of avenues to teach flexibility concepts to prevent boredom and the drudgery of performing the same old stretches day after day. This is also the time to explain the relationship between flexibility exercises performed in class with the back-saver sit-and-reach test and shoulder-stretch test (*FITNESSGRAM*) performed during the fitness assessment portion of your program. When teaching flexibility concepts, stress safety and proper technique. Students should use slow, controlled movements when stretching, holding each stretch to the point of mild discomfort (and perhaps backing off slightly) for 10 to 30 seconds. Holding the stretch at the point of discomfort and backing off slightly ensure application of the overload principle.

Other safety precautions include the following:

- Avoid locking any joint (soft knees, soft joints).
- Do not overstretch a joint (pay attention to the tightness felt during the stretch).
- Never stretch the neck or spine too far.
- Do not perform ballistic stretches (reserved for controlled, sport-specific training of secondary students and adults).
- A trained health care professional should check a student who has excessive mobility.

Along with these safety precautions, be aware of questionable exercises or contraindicated exercises as presented in *Physical Education for Lifelong Fitness: The Physical Best Teacher's Guide, Second Edition*.

Flexibility is an important component of health-related fitness, so resist the temptation to always relegate it to warm-ups and cool-downs. The activities that follow provide many opportunities to use flexibility as the focus of your lesson or add variety to your warm-ups and cool-downs.

Motor Skill Development Through Flexibility Activities

Normal full range of motion (ROM) is essential to learning and perfecting motor skills, and a student with limited ROM will have difficulty mastering a motor skill that a classmate with normal mobility will learn easily. The specificity principle applies here. For example, if a student wants to be able to punt a football or perform a high kick in a soccer game, he or she must have good leg flexibility. Good flexibility, then, enhances motor-skill development. Motor-skill development through fitness activity is the perfect area for you to consider the abilities and disabilities of all students. Some are high achievers, others are low achievers, and still others have physical or intellectual disabilities. Provide opportunities for all students to develop physical skills and be successful in your classroom. If a student is severely disabled, you may need to contact a person who specializes in adapted physical education for assistance in developing an individualized education plan. When students see the connections between flexibility and the physical activities that they are engaging in, they are more likely to continue working on enhancing flexibility as a lifestyle choice. In short, you create a deeper awareness of the need for flexibility.

Flexibility Newsletter

Use the Flexibility Newsletter (located on the CD-ROM) to introduce, reinforce, and extend the concepts behind developing and maintaining good flexibility. The following are ways you might consider using this tool:

- Send the newsletter home as a parent-involvement tool during a mini-unit focusing on flexibility.
- Use the newsletter to help you feature flexibility as the "Health-Related Fitness Component of the Month."
- Introduce the activity ideas as a whole-group task. Ask students to choose one to perform outside class in the next week. They should report their progress through a log, journal, a parent's signature on the newsletter, or other means.
- Validate and promote student involvement in physical activity outside class time and the school setting.
- Among students who can read, promote reading to learn across your curriculum, further supporting the elementary school mission.
- Use the newsletter as a model or springboard to create your own newsletters, tailored specifically to your students' needs.

Feel free to use the Flexibility Newsletter in a way that helps you teach more effectively to the specific needs of your students and their parents.

Activities

Chapter 5 Activities Grid

Activity number	Activity title	Activity page	Concept	Primary	Intermediate	Reproducible (on CD-ROM)
5.1	Human Alphabet Stretch	**104**	Definition	●		None
5.2	Flexible Fun	**106**	Definition		●	Definition Cards
5.3	Beginning Yoga Poses	**108**	Health benefits	●		Beginning Yoga Pose Cards
						Flexibility Health Benefits Poster
5.4	Intermediate Yoga Poses	**110**	Health benefits		●	Intermediate Yoga Pose Cards
						Flexibility Health Benefits Poster
5.5	Bend, Stretch, and Move With Ease	**112**	Warm-up cool down	●		None
5.6	Mirror and Match	**114**	Warm-up cool down		●	None
5.7	Flexibility Activity Picture Chart	**116**	Frequency	●		Flexibility Activity Picture Chart
5.8	Flexibility Activity Log	**118**	Frequency		●	Flexibility Activity Log
5.9	At Least 10 Alligators	**120**	Time	●		At Least 10 Alligators Sign
						At Least 10 Alligators Stretch Cards
						Stretching Reminders
5.10	Roll the Stretch	**122**	Type, or specificity	●	●	Stretching Picture Charts
						Roll the Stretch Assessment Rubric
						Roll the Stretch Teacher Assessment Rubric
5.11	Sport-Specific Stretch Sentence	**124**	Type, or specificity		●	Sport-Specific Stretch Worksheet
5.12	Flexibility FITT Log	**126**	Progression		●	Flexibility FITT Log
						Flexibility FITT Log Worksheet

5.1 Human Alphabet Stretch

PRIMARY LEVEL

Flexibility is the ability to easily bend, stretch, and twist the body.

PURPOSE

■ The student will recognize that the body is capable of a wide range of movement, requiring bending, stretching, and twisting at many joints. The range of motion depends on the joints and the muscles' ability to stretch.

■ Students will explore a variety of stretching positions while learning where joints bend.

RELATIONSHIP TO NATIONAL STANDARDS

Physical Education Standard 6: The student values physical activity for health, enjoyment, challenge, self-expression, and/or social interaction.

EQUIPMENT

■ Laminated alphabet letters (optional, not provided on CD-ROM)

■ Music and player (optional)

Reproducible

None

PROCEDURE

1. Define flexibility. Bring in photos of activities that need flexibility for proper performance, or brainstorm a list with students. This activity will challenge students to perform a stretch in the form of an alphabet letter for at least eight counts. Doing several letters and increasing the number of counts will increase their flexibility during the activity.

2. Have each student find a personal space and move around the activity area until you give a signal to stop.

3. Explain that students will stop on a signal and with their bodies form the letter that you show. An option is to play music while the students are moving and stop the music as the signal to stop and stretch.

4. Repeat as often as desired.

You can try this variation of the previous procedure:

1. Place the letters around the perimeter of the activity space.

2. Place students at the letters (one or more student per letter, depending on class size).

3. Have students make the shape of that letter and then move on to the next letter in the alphabet, for a specified time or until each student has completed the alphabet.

4. Provide an alphabet sheet for students if they need it.

TEACHING HINTS

- This activity assumes that the students are at least somewhat familiar with the alphabet. Most children may be able to form the letter. Extend the activity by having small groups work together to form cooperative group letter shapes.

- Ask students to bring their spelling lists from the classroom. Use these lists to spell words to reinforce memorization or spelling.

- Have the children spell in upper- and lower-case letters.

- Set a time limit on making the letters.

SAMPLE INCLUSION TIP

Children with physical disabilities can make shapes of the letters with the most appropriate body parts in light of their specific disabilities and/or can work with a peer to form the letters.

ASSESSMENT

- Have students tell you one thing that they are able to do when they are flexible.
- Have students tell you two alphabet letters that use a lot of flexibility when playing the Human Alphabet Stretch game.
- Cut out or draw a picture of an activity that uses good flexibility.

5.2 Flexible Fun

INTERMEDIATE LEVEL

Flexibility is the ability to bend, stretch and twist the body with ease, through a full range of motion.

PURPOSE

Students will learn or review the definition of flexibility as a component of health-related fitness.

RELATIONSHIP TO NATIONAL STANDARDS

Physical Education Standard 4: The student achieves and maintains a health-enhancing level of physical fitness.

Physical Education Standard 5: The student exhibits responsible personal and social behavior that respects self and others in physical activity settings.

EQUIPMENT NEEDED

Mats (optional)

PROCEDURE

1. Print the Definition Cards available on the CD-ROM. These cards contain the definition for each component of health-related fitness. Cut each segment into strips, and laminate them. For the activity, you will need one set of flexibility definition cards for each group of students. Choose how many sets of the other cards you wish to use. Scatter the Definition Cards face down in the center of the activity space.

2. Ask students to define flexibility as a component of health-related fitness, or offer the definition for flexibility provided by Physical Best—Flexibility is the ability to bend, stretch, and twist the body with ease, through a full range of motion. Briefly, brainstorm examples of how flexibility helps us in sports, other physical activities, and daily life. Also review the definitions for the other components of health-related fitness (as provided on the Definition Cards).

3. Divide students into small groups of four or five students per group, and have them form relay lines.

4. On your signal, one student from each group runs out and picks up a Definition Card, and runs back to the group. The group then determines whether the words are part of the flexibility definition, and part of the definition that is still needed. If

Reproducible

■ Definition Cards

Flexibility

The ability to bend, stretch,

and twist the body with ease

through a full range of motion

not, the next runner returns the card, places it face down, and picks up another card.

5. The relay continues until the group has all of the word cards needed to complete the definition for flexibility. Then they put the cards in the correct order, and raise their hands to signal that their group is finished.

6. This activity can be used as part of a warm-up, and completed by finishing the activity with a group stretch.

TEACHING HINTS

- When first introducing the activity, you may want to provide each group with the definition of flexibility and/or place the cards face up.
- If using the activity as a warm-up, consider substituting a locomotor more suitable for a warm-up, such as a fast walk.
- Use this activity when teaching the other components of fitness as well.
- Strongly emphasize safety whenever stretching. Never encourage competition among students or groups.
- For all class flexibility activities, always strive to relate stretching to other activities students are interested in or must do (for example, favorite sports or other physical activities and everyday life activities).

SAMPLE INCLUSION TIP

Substitute locomotor movements and adjust placement of cards for students with limited mobility.

ASSESSMENT

- Ask students for an oral or written definition of flexibility.
- Offer an oral or written list of the definitions (but not terms) of muscular strength and endurance, aerobic fitness, and flexibility. Ask students to identify which definition describes flexibility.
- Have students apply the definition of flexibility to themselves by having them record in their journals how flexibility may help them in their favorite physical activity or required daily activities. Repeat this assessment periodically throughout the school year to monitor how students are assimilating the information into their lives.

5.3 Beginning Yoga Poses

PRIMARY LEVEL

Health benefits—Good flexibility can have many health benefits, such as helping with good posture and helping to feel relaxed.

PURPOSE

Students will identify several benefits of using yoga as a way to increase flexibility for a healthy, active life.

RELATIONSHIP TO NATIONAL STANDARDS

Physical Education Standard 6: The student values physical activity for health, enjoyment, challenge, self-expression, and/or social interaction.

Health Education Standard 3: The student will demonstrate the ability to practice health-enhancing behaviors and reduce health risks.

EQUIPMENT

- Soft music and player
- Mats, if desired

PROCEDURE

1. Explain to students that many of the balances and stretches in which we participate during physical education are similar to yoga. Yoga offers many benefits also associated with good flexibility (read Flexibility Health Benefits Poster or the following list):
   - Increased flexibility
   - Increased oxygen because of breathing deeply
   - Increased blood flow

Reproducibles

- Beginning Yoga Pose Cards
- Flexibility Health Benefits Poster

Mountain

In a standing position, place your feet together. Then work on posture with your head, shoulders, hips, and feet in alignment.

Activity 5.3 Beginning Yoga Pose Cards
From *Physical Best activity guide (Elementary level, 2nd edition, by NASPE, 2005, Champaign, IL: Human Kinetics.

Flexibility Health Benefits

- Increased flexibility
- Increased ability to focus
- Increased ability to think clearer and make better decisions
- Decreased muscle tension and increased relaxation
- Greater ease of movement
- Improved coordination
- Reduced risk of injury
- Better body awareness and postural alignment
- Improved circulation and air exchange
- Smoother and easier contractions
- Decreased muscle soreness
- Improved personal appearance and self-image
- Facilitates the development and maintenance of motor skills

Activity 5.3 Flexibility Health Benefits Poster
From *Physical Best activity guide (Elementary level, 2nd edition, by NASPE, 2005, Champaign, IL: Human Kinetics.

- Increased ability to focus
- Increased ability to think clearer and make better decisions

2. Select, or have a student select, a yoga picture.

3. Talk students into position, how to balance, and where to focus.

4. Encourage students to feel their chests rise and fall with their breathing.

5. Repeat with the selection of a new picture.

TEACHING HINTS

- ■ Make yoga fun for primary students by using the imagery of the pose.
- ■ Show the classroom teachers the poses so that the class can have a yoga moment before or after an intense activity in the room, such as a test.

SAMPLE INCLUSION TIP

Try to offer poses and modifications that will be appropriate for the students in your classes with disabilities. For example, allow students to use a wall or chair for balance and support as needed.

ASSESSMENT

- ■ Have the students demonstrate a pose they like, and tell you what part(s) of the body it stretches.
- ■ Ask students to state one benefit of good flexibility.

5.4 Intermediate Yoga Poses

INTERMEDIATE LEVEL

Health benefits—Good flexibility has many health benefits, such as reduced tension and improved posture.

PURPOSE

Students will become aware of the benefits of flexibility in a variety of poses.

RELATIONSHIP TO NATIONAL STANDARDS

Physical Education Standard 6: The student values physical activity for health, enjoyment, challenge, self-expression, and/or social interaction.

Health Education Standard 3: The student will demonstrate the ability to practice health-enhancing behaviors and reduce health risks.

EQUIPMENT

- Soft music and player
- Mats, if desired

PROCEDURE

1. Explain to students that many of the balances and stretches in which we participate during physical education are similar to yoga and that practicing yoga can assist in gaining the benefits of flexibility (display Flexibility Health Benefits Poster).

2. Tell students that everyone has a different flexibility potential. Emphasize that they should not feel pain when stretching or holding a pose.

3. Select, or have a student select, a yoga picture.

4. Talk students into position, how to balance, and where to focus.

Reproducibles

- Intermediate Yoga Pose Cards
- Flexibility Health Benefits Poster

Warrior (Hero)

Turn one foot out to the side. Stretch both arms out, palms down, and lower your shoulders away from your ears. Bend the knee on same side as the turned foot (keep it over the ankle). The other leg is strong and straight. Look over the fingertips of the hand raised over the turned foot. Do the other side.

Activity 5.4 Intermediate Yoga Pose Cards
From *Physical Best activity guide: Elementary level*, 2nd edition, by NASPE, 2005, Champaign, IL: Human Kinetics.

Flexibility Health Benefits

- **Increased flexibility**
- **Increased ability to focus**
- **Increased ability to think clearer and make better decisions**
- **Decreased muscle tension and increased relaxation**
- **Greater ease of movement**
- **Improved coordination**
- **Reduced risk of injury**
- **Better body awareness and postural alignment**
- **Improved circulation and air exchange**
- **Smoother and easier contractions**
- **Decreased muscle soreness**
- **Improved personal appearance and self-image**
- **Facilitates the development and maintenance of motor skills**

Activity 5.4 Flexibility Health Benefits Poster
From *Physical Best activity guide: Elementary level*, 2nd edition, by NASPE, 2005, Champaign, IL: Human Kinetics.

5. Encourage students to feel their chests rise and fall as they breathe in and out.

6. To work on the ability to focus, students should be very quiet as they do the poses.

7. Repeat with the selection of a new picture.

TEACHING HINTS

- For stress management, students need to be quiet and ignore distractions around them.

- Once you have introduced students to the poses, this could be a station activity.

- Talk to the classroom teachers about using yoga on stressful test days before testing to help students relax and focus. Yoga can also be beneficial after testing.

- **Caution:** Students of this age tend to try to impress each other by outdoing one another. A reminder from the teacher about the importance of being aware of your own sensations and not pushing yourself to the point of pain or great discomfort might help.

- Teach students to exhale when moving into a stretch and to use the exhalation to push the stretch a little farther. This method will help them overload their muscles slowly to increase range of motion and will enhance the health benefit of relaxation. Inhaling deeply in the rest phase of multiple stretch repetitions takes the relaxation aspect even further.

- Have students teach their parents, babysitters, or grandparents a yoga pose that could enhance their health-related fitness.

SAMPLE INCLUSION TIP

Provide the opportunity for students with disabilities to practice poses and adaptations prior to class.

ASSESSMENT

- Ask students how they could use yoga to help maintain health-related fitness.
- Ask students to explain how yoga can help increase flexibility.

5.5 Bend, Stretch, and Move With Ease

PRIMARY LEVEL

A **warm-up** gets your body ready for activity. Slow and steady stretching is an important part of a proper warm-up, helping to prevent strains by increasing the elasticity of the muscles and tendons. A **cool-down** helps the body slow down gradually following activity. Slow and steady stretching is also an important part of a proper cool-down, reducing the chances of suffering tight, sore muscles.

PURPOSE

Students will identify stretching as an important part of a proper warm-up and cool-down.

RELATIONSHIP TO NATIONAL STANDARDS

Physical Education Standard 3: The student exhibits a physically active lifestyle.

EQUIPMENT

Tambourine

Reproducible

None

PROCEDURE

1. Take a piece of uncooked spaghetti and try to bend it. Then show how cooked spaghetti bends, stretches, and twists with ease! Why? Unlike the uncooked noodle, it has been warmed up in hot water. Relate these images to what happens to cold versus warm muscles when they are stretched.

2. Students move throughout the activity area in open spaces. Choose a variety of locomotor movements for them to practice. Start with slower movements (such as a walk) and progress to faster movements (such as a skip or jog). Each time you signal the students to stop, lead them through a series of bending, stretching, or twisting activities (move, bend, move, stretch, move, twist, and so on). Use the tambourine to signal changes between the bending, stretching, and twisting activities.

3. Bend one body part and have the students name the body part. Try combinations of body parts.

4. Stretch a muscle or muscle group. Have the students name the muscle or muscle group.

5. Ask students if they can twist from a standing position and from sitting position. (Flexible people can bend, stretch, and twist with ease!)

6. For a cool-down, have students repeat the activity at the end of the period, finishing with slower locomotor movements and easy stretches.

TEACHING HINTS

Add some creative opportunities for older students. Can they move using levels and pathways? Let students choose their favorite sport or activity and have them demonstrate a favorite lower body and upper body stretch for the sport or activity.

SAMPLE INCLUSION TIP

Use resistance bands for stretching when the class is performing a stretch that a particular student may not be able to perform. If needed, secure one end of the resistance band.

ASSESSMENT

© Human Kinetics

- Remind students of the important role that stretching plays in a safe approach to being physically active. Ask questions such as the following: "Why do you warm up before you stretch?" and "Why is it a good idea to stretch at the end of an activity?" Encourage students to make a habit of stretching before and after physical activity.

- Have students teach a family member two of the stretches they learned in class and report on the experience.

- Ask students to demonstrate a (safe!) bending movement, a stretching movement, and a twisting movement.

5.6   Mirror and Match

INTERMEDIATE LEVEL

A **warm-up** gets your body ready for activity. Slow and steady stretching is an important part of a proper warm-up, helping to prevent strains by increasing the elasticity of the muscles and tendons. A **cool-down** helps the body slow down gradually following activity. Slow and steady stretching is also an important part of a proper cool-down, reducing the chances of suffering tight, sore muscles..

PURPOSE

The purpose of the activity is to identify stretching as an important part of a warm-up and cool-down.

RELATIONSHIP TO NATIONAL STANDARDS

Physical Education Standard 1: The student demonstrates competency in motor skills and movement patterns needed to perform a variety of physical activities.

Physical Education Standard 5: The student exhibits responsible personal and social behavior that respects self and others in physical activity settings.

EQUIPMENT

Music of varying tempos and player

Reproducible

None

PROCEDURE

1. Go over the definitions of mirroring and matching. (*Mirroring* means to face the lead partner and reproduce the partner's movement as if looking into a mirror. *Matching* is to duplicate a partner's movement at the same time as they are performing that movement. Therefore, if the lead partner stretches his or her left hand toward the ceiling, the other partner stretches his or her left hand.) Tell the students that on your signal, this is how they will be stretching with their partner during the activity, and to be creative and stretch in ways that help them move during normal activity, as well as in games, dance, or gymnastics.

2. Direct students to find a spot in general space.

3. Start music with a lively tempo and tell students to walk around the space. Stop the music, and direct them to slow down and approach another student and touch the toe of one foot to the toes of one foot of the other student (toe to toe). Ask students to decide who will be a one and who will be a two.

4. Tell number ones to start "Mirroring" and number twos to follow them. Play music with a slower tempo during this time, while directing the children to move slowly with the music.

5. Start the lively tempo again, and direct students to skip through general space. Stop the music and ask the partners to pair up again, this time with partner two becoming the lead partner, and the lead partner leading a "Matching" stretch to the slower tempo.

6. Repeat steps 3 to 5, students can keep or change partners for the next round of mirroring and matching, and continue to use a sequence of more intense locomotors such as jogging and galloping.

7. Reverse the locomotive choices for a cool-down.

TEACHING HINTS

Cue students to perform stretches on the ground or standing up.

SAMPLE INCLUSION TIP

To increase the intensity of the movement for a student in a wheelchair, an ergometer could be used when moving in general space.

ASSESSMENT

- Ask questions about specific muscle groups that they should warm up and cool down (upper body, head, legs, and backside). What are the names of the muscles that they stretched?

- Ask students to volunteer to demonstrate some of the movements they came up with that gave them the best stretches, and to name the body part(s) stretched.

5.7 Flexibility Activity Picture Chart

PRIMARY LEVEL

Frequency is number of times per week that you need to stretch for good flexibility. Experts recommend that to make and keep your body flexible you should stretch at least three times a week.

PURPOSE

Students will understand and participate in stretching activities at least three times a week.

RELATIONSHIP TO NATIONAL STANDARDS

Physical Education Standard 3: The student participates regularly in physical activity.

Health Education Standard 3: The student will demonstrate the ability to practice health-enhancing behaviors and reduce health risks.

EQUIPMENT

Pencils

PROCEDURE

1. Have the students brainstorm ways that they stretch in their everyday lives. Encourage them to use examples from outside physical education class.

2. Pass out the Flexibility Activity Picture Chart, explain how to fill it out, and ask students to work with their parents at home to fill it out for the next one to two weeks.

TEACHING HINTS

■ Encourage students to find different ways to stay flexible. Give them examples that fit within their community.

■ Construct a bulletin board with hand-drawn or magazine pictures of the different activities that the students found to do.

■ Have a family day in physical education when family members join the students in activities that the family can do at home to keep in shape.

■ You may want to complete a chart to show the students as an example.

SAMPLE INCLUSION TIP

Use this activity as an opportunity for diversity training. Have students with disabilities share or demonstrate the activities they participate in outside of school.

Reproducible

■ Flexibility Activity Picture Chart

Name: _____ Class: _____ Date: _____

Activity 5.7
Flexibility Activity Picture Chart

Circle the activities that you have done in the past week or in a blank space draw another activity that you have done. How many days did you do this? If it is more than one, write that number by the picture.

Activity 5.7 Flexibility Activity Picture Chart
From *Physical Best activity guide: Elementary level*, 2nd edition, by NASPE, 2005, Champaign, IL: Human Kinetics.

ASSESSMENT

- Have students tell you how many days per week they perform flexibility activities.

- Have students name a flexibility activity that they could do every day.

- Collect the homework sheet and lead a class discussion on the activities circled and added.

- Have students discuss their favorite flexibility activity with the class.

© Human Kinetics

5.8 Flexibility Activity Log

INTERMEDIATE LEVEL

Frequency is number of times per week that you need to stretch for good joint flexibility. Experts recommend that to make and keep your body flexible you should stretch at least three times a week.

PURPOSE

Students will understand and participate in stretching activities and tasks at least three times a week.

RELATIONSHIP TO NATIONAL STANDARDS

Physical Education Standard 3: The student participates regularly in physical activity.

Health Education Standard 3: The student will demonstrate the ability to practice health-enhancing behaviors and reduce health risks.

EQUIPMENT

Pencils

PROCEDURE

1. Have the students brainstorm some ways that they stretch in their everyday lives. Encourage them to use examples from outside physical education class.

2. Pass out the Flexibility Activity Log, explain how to fill it out, and ask them to work with their parents at home to fill it out for the next one to two weeks.

TEACHING HINTS

- Encourage students to find different ways to stay active. Give them examples that fit within their community.
- Construct a bulletin board with hand-drawn or magazine pictures of the different activities that the students found to do.
- Have a family day in physical education when family members join students in activities that the family can do at home to keep in shape.

SAMPLE INCLUSION TIP

Provide parents and students with a list of agencies (departments of parks and recreation or therapeutic recreation programs) that offer a variety of programs for students with disabilities outside of the school environment.

Reproducible

- Flexibility Activity Log

Name: _____ Class: _____ Date: _____

Activity 5.8
Flexibility Activity Log

Date	Description of activity (what kind)	Time (how long)	Your initials

Activity 5.8 Flexibility Activity Log
From *Physical Best activity guide: Elementary level,* 2nd edition, by NASPE, 2005, Champaign, IL: Human Kinetics.

© Human Kinetics

ASSESSMENT

■ Have students tell or write a definition of frequency and how many days per week they should participate in flexibility activities

■ Collect the homework sheet and lead a class discussion on the activities.

■ Have students discuss their favorite flexibility activity with the class.

5.9

At Least 10 Alligators

PRIMARY LEVEL

Time is how long you need to hold a stretch to improve or maintain flexibility. Experts recommend that you hold each stretch, without bouncing or jerking, for 10 seconds (progressing to 30 seconds).

PURPOSE

Students will demonstrate an understanding that to stretch safely they must not bounce and that to improve or maintain flexibility they must hold stretches for 10 seconds or longer.

RELATIONSHIP TO NATIONAL STANDARDS

Physical Education Standard 4: The student achieves and maintains a health-enhancing level of physical fitness.

Health Education Standard 1: The student will comprehend concepts related to health promotion and disease prevention.

EQUIPMENT

None

PROCEDURE

1. Instruct students about the importance of not bouncing or jerking as they perform each stretch. Remind students that everyone has a different level of flexibility and

Reproducibles

■ At Least 10 Alligators Sign
■ At Least 10 Alligators Stretch Cards
■ Stretching Reminders

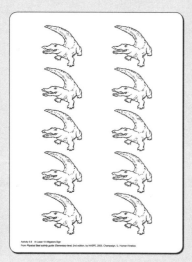

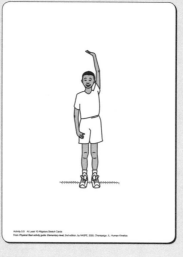

Stretching Reminders

1. Never bounce when stretching
2. Never hold your breath when stretching. Inhale and exhale.
3. Never lock your joints when stretching.
4. Don't extend your joints too far when stretching.
5. Always hold the stretch for 10 to 30 seconds.
6. The stretch should never hurt.
7. Don't pull on your joints.

that they should not compare their bodies to the bodies of other. They should not stretch to a point of undue discomfort. Tell them that today they will practice holding stretches for at least 10 seconds.

2. On your signal, students move in an activity area using a locomotor skill.

3. On the signal "Stop!" students freeze and ask you, "What do you see?" As you show the sign they respond, "At least 10 alligators."

4. Immediately after they say, "At least 10 alligators," you assume a stretch position of your choice, or hold up one of the "At Least 10 Alligators"

Stretch Cards for a specific group of muscles. Then the students take the position. You cue the students to count the alligators by saying, "One alligator, two alligators, three alligators . . ." until they reach 10.

5. Repeat the activity by choosing another locomotor pattern, calling, "Stop," and ask, "What do you see?" They respond the same way by saying, "One alligator . . ."

TEACHING HINTS

■ Monitor students closely to ensure that they do not bounce or jerk when stretching. Invite students who are stretching correctly to demonstrate for others.

■ Create a bulletin board depicting pictures of various stretch poses. The title of the board could be "At Least 10 Alligators," and numbers 1 through 10 could connect the pictures.

■ Explain to students that the first *T* in FITT stands for time. Remind them to hold stretching activities for at least 10 seconds, gradually working up to 30 seconds. Turn the first *T* on the FITT bulletin board into "Time = How Long!" Place a clock on the bulletin board next to the *T* for time.

SAMPLE INCLUSION TIP

Allow students to vary the locomotor and modify the stretch as needed. Use peer assistance when possible.

ASSESSMENT

■ Ask students how long they should hold a stretch position.

■ Have students demonstrate other stretches. Each stretch should last for at least 10 seconds and be free of bouncing and jerking.

5.10 Roll the Stretch

PRIMARY AND INTERMEDIATE LEVELS

Specificity, or **type,** in relation to flexibility means that only the joint and muscle group that you are stretching will become more flexible. That is, if you do stretching activities for your arms, your legs will not become more flexible.

PURPOSE

- Students will understand that there are many different muscle groups that need to be stretched.
- Students will understand that stretches are "specific" to particular muscle groups.

RELATIONSHIP TO NATIONAL STANDARDS

Physical Education Standard 4: The student achieves and maintains a health-enhancing level of physical fitness.

Health Education Standard 3: The student will demonstrate the ability to practice health-enhancing behaviors and reduce health risks.

EQUIPMENT

- A pair of dice per group
- Relaxing music and player

Reproducibles

- Stretching Picture Charts, one per group
- Roll the Stretch Assessment Rubric (intermediate only)
- Roll the Stretch Teacher Assessment Rubric (intermediate only)

1. Feet and ankles
2. Lower legs
3. Hamstrings
4. Adductors
5. Quadriceps
6. Hips and gluteus muscles

Name: _____ Class: _____ Date: _____

Activity 5.10
Roll the Stretch
Assessment Rubric

How did you do today?
Always = 3
Most of the time = 2
Sometimes = 1

Name	Always	Most of the time	Sometimes
On task stretching			
Cooperated with everyone			
Slow and steady movements			

Activity 5.10
Roll the Stretch
Teacher Assessment Rubric

Always = 3
Most of the time = 2
Sometimes = 1

	Group 1	Group 2	Group 3	Group 4	Group 5	Group 6
On task stretching						
Cooperated with everyone						
Slow and steady movements						
Comments						

PROCEDURE

1. Have students participate in an activity that will warm up their bodies and prepare them for stretching.

2. Divide students into small groups (for intermediate students, assign each group a group number on your teacher assessment rubric). Give each group a stretching chart and a pair of dice.

3. Explain that they will use a slow, steady movement when performing all stretches, to help prevent injury.

4. One student rolls the dice and reads the number. That student then locates the picture on the chart. With a slow, steady count (30 seconds), the student leads the group in performing the stretch.

5. The chart and dice are then passed to the next student, who becomes the roller and leader.

6. Make sure that all students have a chance to lead.

7. For intermediate level students, the teacher circulates around the activity space, assessing students with the teacher rubric. Upon completion of the activity, the intermediate students should also complete the student rubric.

TEACHING HINTS

■ Perform the activity as a class for the first lesson and in small groups for the second lesson.

■ Ask the leaders to count softly aloud so that you can hear if they are speeding up.

■ To help prevent overuse of one muscle group, have students reroll the dice if the same exercise number comes up twice in a row.

SAMPLE INCLUSION TIPS

■ Place the music in a location where the child with an attention deficit can hear soothing sounds that will help him or her be able to do slow, steady stretches.

■ Secure a resistance band for student that is not able to perform the designated stretch.

■ Teacher can provide two stretches for each body part and allow the student to choose one of the stretches (be conscious of meeting the needs of all students).

ASSESSMENT

■ Select a body part or muscle group and ask students to demonstrate or write a stretch for that body part.

■ Use the student and teacher rubrics to assess intermediate students and groups—discuss results.

5.11 Sport-Specific Stretch Sentence

INTERMEDIATE LEVEL

Specificity, or **type,** in relation to flexibility means that only the joint and muscle group that you are stretching will become more flexible. That is, if you do stretching activities for your arms, your legs will not become more flexible.

PURPOSE

- Students will demonstrate that the specific joints and muscle groups that they stretch will become more flexible.
- Students will explore stretching to prepare for specific sports activities.

RELATIONSHIP TO NATIONAL STANDARDS

Physical Education Standard 2: The student will demonstrate understanding of movement concepts, principles, strategies, and tactics as they apply to the learning and performance of physical activities.

Health Education Standard 1: The student will comprehend concepts related to health promotion and disease prevention.

EQUIPMENT

- Pencils
- Elementary writing paper, cut into strips of two or three lines each (cut along solid lines)

PROCEDURE

1. Instruct students about the importance of not bouncing or jerking as they perform each stretch. Remind them that everyone has a different level of flexibility and that they should not compare their bodies to the bodies of others.

2. Review common stretches used to prepare the body to play sports and other activities. You can use the stretch pictures provided on the Sport-Specific Stretch Worksheet.

3. Review the correct form for constructing a sentence and tell students that the sentence they are creating will have three specific stretches for their sport.

4. Divide the class into groups of two or three students per group, and give them a copy of the stretch pictures, a pencil, and their sentence strip or writing paper. You can assign the same sport for each group, or assign them different sports.

5. The students should choose three flexibility exercises that stretch out the body

Reproducible

- Sport-Specific Stretch Worksheet

Neck stretch
Cross-chest stretch
Heel stretch
On the floor gluteus muscle stretches
Triceps stretch
Floor hamstring pull
Quadriceps stretch
Butterfly stretch
Arms clasped behind back
Straddle stretch

for the particular sport they were given (basketball for example, might include a shoulder stretch for shooting and dribbling, and a quadriceps/hip flexor stretch and a calf stretch for jumping and running).

6. Ask students to write a sentence that explains a sport-specific stretch routine, using the flexibility exercises (basketball sentence example: To prepare for basketball, I will warm-up and then stretch out, by stretching my shoulders, thighs, and calves).

7. Once completed, each group leads the class through their stretch sentence (holding each stretch as they get to it, for 10 seconds). If the class is not already warmed up, first lead them through one or more locomotor movements or patterns commonly used in that sport.

TEACHING HINTS

▪ Monitor students closely to ensure that they do not bounce or jerk when stretching.

▪ To further challenge the students, and make the activity more active, have them select two locomotor patterns common to their sport (basketball, for example, could include defensive slides and back pedaling). Have them alternate stretches with locomotors when constructing their sentence.

▪ Lay poly spots around the activity space (with adequate room to move between each) and have each group select a spot.

▪ Create a FITT bulletin board, and explain that the second *T* in FITT stands for type, or specificity. Include stretches for specific muscle groups used in sports or activities.

▪ Remind students that they should stretch specifically for the type of sport or activity that they will be performing.

SAMPLE INCLUSION TIP

Have groups work to create adaptations to stretches for a specified sport and disability.

ASSESSMENT

▪ Ask students the names of the muscles that stretch specific body parts.

▪ Have students demonstrate the movement sentence to their class and discuss their choices in relation to a sport.

▪ Ask students how long they should hold a stretch position to improve flexibility.

5.12 Flexibility FITT Log

INTERMEDIATE LEVEL

Progression refers to how an individual should increase overload. Proper progression involves a gradual increase in the level of exercise that is manipulated by increasing either frequency, intensity, or time, or a combination of all three components. The **overload principle** states that a body system (cardiorespiratory, muscular, or skeletal) must perform at a level beyond normal in order to adapt and improve physiological function and fitness.

PURPOSE

Students will learn and apply the training principles of progression and overload to flexibility by completing a FITT Log and Worksheet.

RELATIONSHIP TO NATIONAL STANDARDS

Physical Education Standard 3: The student participates regularly in physical activity.

Physical Education Standard 4: The student achieves and maintains a health-enhancing level of physical fitness.

Health Education Standard 3: The student will demonstrate the ability to practice health-enhancing behaviors and reduce health risks.

EQUIPMENT

Pencils

PROCEDURE

1. Briefly review the two-word definitions of the aspects of FITT—frequency (how often), intensity (how hard), time (how long), and type (what kind).

Reproducibles

■ Flexibility FITT Log

■ Flexibility FITT Log Worksheet

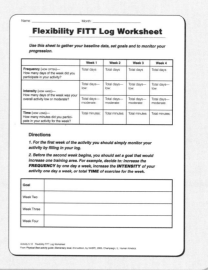

2. Ask students to offer brief examples of how they have applied the FITT Guidelines to flexibility in previous health-related fitness activities.

3. Share descriptions of the concepts of progression and overload.

4. Distribute one blank Flexibility FITT Log to each student. Review each category and how it relates to FITT. Outline how students can apply progression as they use the form.

5. Ask class to share flexibility activities, and to choose two to three stretches for various body parts, and write them on the "Activity selected" line of their log.

6. Have each student write their name on the log.

7. Assign students to log their flexibility physical activity performed outside class for one week.

8. Have students fill in one week of the Flexibility FITT Log.

9. Guide students in setting goals for progression and overload and write them on the Flexibility FITT Log Worksheet.

10. At the end of each week, meet and discuss their progress and set new goals.

TEACHING HINTS

- Ask students at each class meeting how their logs are coming along.
- Require parent or guardian initials if necessary to encourage participation.
- Ask the school's after-school care providers to provide space, time, and other support for students to add to their logs.
- Tie in the *FITNESSGRAM* flexibility assessments.

SAMPLE INCLUSION TIP

Help students with special circumstances come up with alternative activities to suit their needs and abilities. You can modify activities suggested earlier in this chapter, provide suggestions for students who must stay indoors because of safety or space constraints, or otherwise help students develop activity ideas that will work for them.

ASSESSMENT

After the month, have students review their logs with you and write about their experience by answering questions such as the following:

- Were you able to safely build up to a higher level of intensity over the course of the month, do the activities more frequently each week, or spend more time doing each activity? Which changes did you make, if any?
- If you were able to make changes, how might the changes have affected your flexibility fitness?
- If you did not make changes, what might you be able to do differently in the future?

Realize that many factors, such as the child's initial level of fitness and participation (if already high, they may not progress for that reason), and other personal factors may affect the answers to these questions. Keeping this in mind, focus on the assessment as a means to teach and reinforce the concepts of progression and overload.

Body Composition

Chapter Contents

- Defining Body Composition
- Relating Body Composition to the Other Health-Related Components
- Nutrition
- Teaching Guidelines for Body Composition
- Body Composition Newsletter
- Activities

The activities in this chapter explore body composition, an important component of fitness. At the elementary level, students should understand the major concepts regarding body composition, including energy intake and expenditure, guidelines for healthy eating such as the Food Guide Pyramid, and factors that affect body composition such as genetics, diet, and physical activity. When completing these activities, students should understand how their behaviors will affect their body composition. The following information introduces the subject of body composition at the elementary level. For more information on this topic, refer to the chapters about body composition and nutrition in *Physical Education for Lifelong Fitness: The Physical Best Teacher's Guide, Second Edition*.

Defining Body Composition

Body composition is the amount of lean body mass (all tissues other than fat, such as bone, muscle, organs, and body fluids) compared with the amount of body fat, usually expressed in terms of percent body fat. Among the common ways of assessing whether body composition is appropriate are BMI-for-age tables, skinfold caliper testing, and waist-to-hip ratio. When assessing body composition in elementary level students, remember that body composition may change rapidly with growth spurts, so an assessment method must accommodate these changes.

Relating Body Composition to the Other Health-Related Components

As with any other component of health-related fitness, a person's body composition does not develop in isolation from the other components. Indeed, you should show students the connections among all health-related fitness components so that they can clearly see how their personal choices affect this area of health-related fitness. Although genetics, environment, and culture play significant roles, body composition results largely from physical activity levels in the other components:

- **aerobic fitness**—Aerobic activities burn calories.
- **muscular strength and endurance**—Muscle cells burn (metabolize) more calories at rest than fat cells do. To increase the likelihood that students will maintain appropriate body composition, emphasize physical activity that follows the principles of training.
- **flexibility**—A flexible body can better tolerate aerobic fitness and muscular strength and endurance activities.

Nutrition

Nutrition also plays an important role in body composition. In addition to reviewing the Food Guide Pyramid, discuss appropriate portion size. In the United States, portion sizes have been increasing for the last three decades. The Western diet includes many highly processed, high-fat, high-sugar, and high-salt foods. The human body was designed to work best with whole grains, vegetables, and fruits.

Nutrients fall into six classes: carbohydrate, protein, fat, vitamins, minerals, and water. Because all are essential for good health, the diet must provide all six.

- Carbohydrate provides most of the energy for people across the world and represents the preferred source of energy for the body. People should obtain carbohydrate from whole grains, cereals, vegetables, and fruits. Refined grains and sugars can also provide carbohydrates.

▥ Protein serves as the structural component for vital body parts. Every cell in the body contains protein. In the United States, meat is the primary source of protein.

▥ Fat serves as a concentrated form of energy, and the human body stores excess calories as fat.

▥ Vitamins and minerals contain no calories, but small amounts are essential for good health.

▥ Many students do not realize that water is an essential nutrient. Students need to drink at least six to eight cups of water daily.

Teaching Guidelines for Body Composition

Approach discussions about body composition objectively and as a topic about which students should be sensitive. Strive to point out connections among physical activity, diet, and body composition related to daily life, recreational activities, and physical education activities. Never use a student as a positive or negative example regarding body composition. Heavier students may become uncomfortable, so be prepared to help them approach this as a learning process, not as a negative or punitive message. Emphasize that a student who is overfat because of genetics can still greatly reduce health risks by being physically active. Remember, students will follow your lead with their peers. If you are comfortable with the topic, they will be too.

Although approaching body composition in the physical education setting can be a delicate matter, you must address this important component of fitness. Handle body composition instruction professionally and by concentrating on how a good diet and active lifestyle can positively affect it. Emphasize that normal bodies comes in all sizes and encourage a positive self-image.

Body Composition Newsletter

Use the Body Composition Newsletter (located on the CD-ROM) to introduce, reinforce, and extend the concepts behind developing and maintaining healthy body composition. The following are ways that you might use this tool:

▥ Send the newsletter home as a parent-involvement tool during a miniunit focusing on body composition.

▥ Use the newsletter to help you feature body composition as the "Health-Related Fitness Component of the Month."

▥ Validate and promote student involvement in physical activity outside class time and the school setting.

▥ Among students who can read, promote reading to learn across your curriculum, further supporting the elementary school mission.

▥ Use the newsletter as a model or springboard to create your own newsletter, tailored specifically to your students' needs.

Feel free to use the Body Composition Newsletter in a way that helps you teach more effectively to the specific needs of your students and their parents.

Activities

Chapter 6 Activities Grid

Activity number	Activity title	Activity page	Concept	Primary	Intermediate	Reproducible (on CD-ROM)
6.1	Maintaining Balance	**132**	Definition	●		Body Composition Benefit Signs
6.2	What's the Mix?	**134**	Definition		●	What's the Mix? Worksheet
6.3	Off the Couch	**136**	Health benefits	●		Clock Illustration
6.4	Everyday Activities	**138**	Health benefits		●	Everyday Activities Station Signs
						Everyday Activities Station Recording Chart
6.5	Little Bird Growing Dance	**140**	Growth and development	●		None
6.6	Nutrition Hunt	**142**	Nutrition	●		Food Guide Pyramid
6.7	Menu Maker	**144**	Nutrition		●	Food Guide Pyramid Worksheet
						Menu Maker Worksheet
6.8	Calorie Burn-Up	**146**	Metabolism	●		None
6.9	Metabolism Medley	**149**	Metabolism		●	Physical Activity Pyramid for Children

6.1

Maintaining Balance

PRIMARY LEVEL

Body composition is the amount of lean body mass (all tissues other than fat, such as bone, muscle, organs, and body fluids) compared with the amount of body fat. A healthy body composition involves having a healthy amount of both lean body mass and fat mass to allow you to enjoy life, be active, and have energy to spare, and grow and develop.

PURPOSE

- Students will learn about healthy body composition.
- Students will engage in critical thinking, use teamwork, and practice following instructions.

RELATIONSHIP TO NATIONAL STANDARDS

Physical Education Standard 4: The student will achieve and maintain a health-enhancing level of physical fitness.

Health Education Standard 1: The student will comprehend concepts related to health promotion and disease prevention.

EQUIPMENT

- 30 to 35 bowling pins
- Two-liter bottles or small cones
- Pinnies for one team, if desired (see Teaching Hints)

PROCEDURE

1. Using the Body Composition Benefits Signs, discuss the benefits of fat and lean body mass, and the importance of a healthy balance between the two.

2. Scatter the pins over the playing area, spacing them as far apart as possible, with half upright and half laying down.

3. Divide the class into two teams—the "Ups-fats" and the "Downs-leans."

4. Line up the teams at opposite ends of the playing area.

5. On the signal, all members of each team try either to set the pins up or to set the pins down, depending on their assignment. After a couple of minutes call a halt and count the number of pins in each position. Record the number of pins down and the number of pins up and keep a total score through several rounds.

6. Switch teams, names, and begin another round.

Reproducible

- Body Composition Benefit Signs

Body Composition:
Benefits of Fat

1. **Acts as an insulator, helping the body adapt to heat and cold**
2. **Acts as a shock absorber, helping to protect internal organs and bones from injury**
3. **Helps the body use vitamins effectively**
4. **Acts as stored energy when the body needs energy**
5. **Maintains healthy skin and hair**
6. **Regulates levels of cholesterol in the blood**

Activity 6.1 Body Composition Benefit Signs
From *Physical Best activity guide: Elementary level*, 2nd edition, by NASPE, 2005, Champaign, IL: Human Kinetics.

---

7. Every time the "Ups-fats" set up a pin, they must circle around the pin two times.

8. Do not tell the students that up and down represent anything until they have completed all the rounds. The next time you play, review and note that the Ups must work harder to "maintain a balance."

9. Continue for several rounds and then follow up with a discussion about maintaining balance. As you switch roles for the teams, the balance of scores at the end of the round will probably shift. You can discuss how our balance also shifts during life with active and inactive periods.

10. In most cases the Leans will win, and you then discuss why they have more energy and how they can get more energy

TEACHING HINTS

- To ensure that the Leans win most of the time, you may want to place two or three more players on their team.

- You can put pinnies on the teams to represent the Ups-fats and the Downs-leans and keep track of who is playing.

- Demand safety. If a student is recklessly knocking cones down, apply a significant consequence.

- If your teams are large, have only half the members go for a minute at a time while the other half circles the perimeter of the activity space as motivators for their teammates.

- Students will remember benefit statements better if they are visual. Use the Body Composition Benefit Signs during the activity as a tool to present the body composition concept of fitness.

SAMPLE INCLUSION TIP

Add rest (safe) areas into the game so that those who need a rest can do so.

ASSESSMENT

- Ask, "Why is it important to have both lean mass and body fat?" (answers include the many health benefits listed on the Body Composition Benefit Signs).

6.2

What's the Mix?

INTERMEDIATE LEVEL

Body composition is the ratio of lean body mass (bone, muscle, organs, and body fluids) to fat. Because lean body mass weighs more than fat, using a scale to determine ideal body composition does not work. A person who is overweight on a scale may actually be in good shape. A person must also avoid having too much fat. Bodies need both lean body mass and fat to function properly.

PURPOSE

- Students will identify that for equal volumes, lean body mass weighs more than body fat.
- Students will learn how to maintain ideal body mass.
- Students will maintain continuous aerobic activity for a specified time.

RELATIONSHIP TO NATIONAL STANDARDS

Physical Education Standard 4: The student achieves and maintains a health-enhancing level of physical fitness.

Health Education Standard 1: The student will comprehend concepts related to health promotion and disease prevention.

EQUIPMENT

- Hula hoops
- Foam balls and bean bags (one foam ball for every four beanbags, enough for at least one set per child)
- Music

PROCEDURE

1. Use two objects that are the same size but different weight to demonstrate that lean mass and fat mass can take up the same space but have different weights (a foam ball and a beanbag work well).

2. Pass the two objects around and explain how our total body weight does not indicate whether or not our body composition is healthy. Ask them which represents fat (foam ball) and which represents lean (beanbag).

3. Explain that today's activity will help students learn more about healthy body composition using foam balls for fat weight and beanbags for lean weight.

4. Divide students into a group of four or five students with one hoop per group.

Reproducible

- What's the Mix? Worksheet

Name: _____ Class: _____ Date: _____

Activity 6.2
What's the Mix?

1. *Five pounds of human fat. Five pounds of human muscle.*
   Which one takes up more space? _____

2. What is the ratio of lean mass to fat called? _____

3. Which weighs more for the same volume—lean mass or fat? _____

4. What are the components of lean mass? _____
   _____

5. What can you do to maintain healthy body composition? _____
   _____

Mix Facts
- Your body needs both lean body mass and fat to function properly.
- Because lean body mass weighs more than fat, you cannot use a scale to determine your ideal body composition!

These two people are overweight on the height and weight tables.

These two people are not overweight on the height and weight tables.

HOWEVER, they have the right amount of fat!

HOWEVER, they have too much fat!

Activity 6.2 What's the Mix? Worksheet
From *Physical Best activity guide: Elementary level*, 2nd edition, by NASPE, 2005, Champaign, IL: Human Kinetics.

5. Place one hoop in the center of the room with many foam balls and beanbags—one foam ball for every four beanbags (an approximate representation of fat to lean weight ratio).

6. On the "Go" signal, all students leave their home hoops to go to some other hoop, that is, the center hoop or some other group's hoop. Students remove one beanbag from a hoop and return it to their hoop, or they may deposit one foam ball into any other group's hoop from the center hoop or their own.

7. Discuss the balance of calories in and calories out and how to achieve it (balance of healthy eating and physical activity).

TEACHING HINTS

■ Provide some basic safety rules before beginning, including the need to stay in personal space, placing and not throwing the objects into the hoop, and not guarding/defending hoops.

■ Stress the importance of working and cooperating as a team.

■ Stress the importance of having more lean body mass on the body compared with fat mass, but remind students that having fat mass is just as important in the functioning of the body (so the hoop should not have zero fat).

■ You can vary this game to demonstrate the balance of carbohydrates, fats, and proteins needed as building blocks for healthy eating.

■ Tie in science by asking the classroom teacher to teach students the difference between weight and mass.

■ Discuss how appearances can be deceptive in judging good health.

■ Design a project (shadow box, bulletin board, HyperCard stack on the computer) that illustrates the definition of body composition and the fact that physical activity helps people reach and maintain a healthy body composition.

SAMPLE INCLUSION TIP

Place objects on a student desk to accommodate those who would find bending difficult.

ASSESSMENT

■ Use the questions on the What's the Mix? Worksheet as a written or an oral assessment.

6.3 Off the Couch

PRIMARY LEVEL

Health benefits—Regular physical activity is a key to maintaining healthy body composition. "Children should accumulate at least 60 minutes, and up to several hours, of age-appropriate physical activity on all, or most days of the week. This daily accumulation should include moderate and vigorous physical activity with the majority of the time being spent in activity that is intermittent in nature" (NASPE 2004).

PURPOSE

- Students will participate in a moderate to vigorous physical activity.
- Students will understand that to help maintain healthy body composition, physical activities should be both aerobic and muscular in nature.

RELATIONSHIP TO NATIONAL STANDARDS

Physical Education Standard 4: The student achieves and maintains a health-enhancing level of physical fitness.

Health Education Standard 1: The student will comprehend concepts related to health promotion and disease prevention.

EQUIPMENT

- Poly spots (at least six per student)
- Upbeat music and music player
- One container per student (paper lunch bag, plastic gallon zip-type, plastic grocery bag, or small bucket)
- Equipment as needed for aerobic and muscular activities

PROCEDURE

1. Scatter poly spots around the activity space.

2. Each student should sit by a container that holds the Clock Illustration (a clock divided into six sections). Explain to the students that they will accumulate physical activity time by moving in and around the poly spots. Discuss the importance of regular physical activity, and that both aerobic and muscular activities contribute to a healthy body composition.

3. Begin the music and direct students to start moving around the activity space, selecting a movement/locomotor.

4. Stop the music and ask students to pick up one poly spot and place it in their container.

Reproducible

- Clock Illustration

5. Start the music again and direct students to again begin moving through the activity space using a different movement/locomotor.

6. Continue until students have collected six poly spots, choosing a variety of movements or locomotors, some which are more aerobic in nature (walking, skipping, and so on) and some of which are more muscular in nature (biceps curls using tennis balls or animal walks). Explain that each poly spot represents 10 minutes of physical activity.

7. Have the students place the Clock Illustrations on the floor and put one poly spot in each 10-minute section to indicate a total of 60 minutes of daily physical activity.

8. When the students repeat the activity, have them play until they have picked up four poly spots. Take out the Clock Illustration again and have the students place a poly spot on four of the 10-minute sections. Have them figure out how many more minutes of activity they would need to perform to meet the recommendation for 60 minutes of daily physical activity.

TEACHING HINTS

■ Enforce safety during movement. You may want to place poly spots in buckets, scattered around the space.

■ When picking up the poly spots, if desired, use the rest period to lead students in stretches. Remind students that stretching helps prevent injury and generally helps us stay more active and able to move freely, which also helps us maintain a healthier body composition.

SAMPLE INCLUSION TIP

Use a beanbag with a beeper for students who are visually impaired. When the student finds the beanbag, trade the beanbag for a poly spot and quickly hide the beanbag with a beeper in another location for the student to find again.

ASSESSMENT

■ Ask or remind students what a "couch potato" is in everyday life and brainstorm with them how they can spend less time like a couch potato and more time staying active through aerobic fitness and muscular fitness activities outside the class setting.

■ Ask what types of physical activities contribute to healthy body composition (aerobic fitness and muscular activities primarily—with flexibility contributing).

■ Revisit this activity on another day, and stop short of collecting six beanbags. Have students calculate how many minutes of activity time their beanbags represent, and how much time they will need to be active through the remainder of the day to reach the 60-minute recommendation. Brainstorm ideas for achieving the recommendation (recess, and so on).

6.4 Everyday Activities

INTERMEDIATE LEVEL

Health benefits—Regular physical activity is a key to maintaining healthy body composition. "Children should accumulate at least 60 minutes, and up to several hours, of age-appropriate physical activity on all, or most, days of the week. This daily accumulation should include moderate and vigorous physical activity with the majority of the time being spent in activity that is intermittent in nature" (NASPE 2004).

PURPOSE

- Students will participate in a number of moderate to vigorous physical activities.
- Students will understand that to help maintain healthy body composition, those activities should be both aerobic and muscular in nature.
- Students will relate everyday activities to physical activity and fitness.

RELATIONSHIP TO NATIONAL STANDARDS

Physical Education Standard 4: The student achieves and maintains a health-enhancing level of physical fitness.

Health Education Standard 1: The student will comprehend concepts related to health promotion and disease prevention.

EQUIPMENT

- Set up a physical activity circuit with a variety of station activities. Use the examples provided on the CD-ROM or develop your own.
- Pencils

PROCEDURE

1. Explain to the students that the objective of this activity is to understand that many different types of physical activity (aerobic and muscular, moderate and vigorous)

Reproducibles

- Everyday Activities Station Signs
- Everyday Activities Station Recording Chart (develop your own if you select alternate activities)

STATION 1

Go for 2

Basketball shooting.

Activity 6.4 Everyday Activities Station Signs
From *Physical Best activity guide: elementary level*, 2nd edition, by NASPE, 2005, Champaign, IL: Human Kinetics.

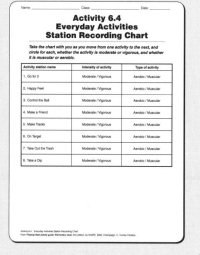

Name: _____ Class: _____ Date: _____

Activity 6.4
Everyday Activities
Station Recording Chart

Take the chart with you as you move from one activity to the next, and circle for each, whether the activity is moderate or vigorous, and whether it is muscular or aerobic.

Activity station name	Intensity of activity	Type of activity
1. Go for 2	Moderate / Vigorous	Aerobic / Muscular
2. Happy Feet	Moderate / Vigorous	Aerobic / Muscular
3. Control the Ball	Moderate / Vigorous	Aerobic / Muscular
4. Make a Friend	Moderate / Vigorous	Aerobic / Muscular
5. Make Tracks	Moderate / Vigorous	Aerobic / Muscular
6. On Target	Moderate / Vigorous	Aerobic / Muscular
7. Take Out the Trash	Moderate / Vigorous	Aerobic / Muscular
8. Take a Dip	Moderate / Vigorous	Aerobic / Muscular

Activity 6.4 Everyday Activities Station Recording Chart
From *Physical Best activity guide: elementary level*, 2nd edition, by NASPE, 2005, Champaign, IL: Human Kinetics.

are good for the body and that each contributes to an active, healthy lifestyle and healthy body composition.

2. Hand out the station recording charts and pencils. Review the station activities.

3. Divide students into small groups and assign one group to each station.

4. Give students two minutes to participate in the physical activity at the station.

5. Have the students think about their breathing rates,

feel their heart rates (on their chests), or take a pulse, if they are able. Students should determine whether the activity at that station was moderate or vigorous, note that judgment on their station recording charts, and then rotate to the next station.

6. Repeat the activity until everyone has visited all stations.

TEACHING HINTS

- Allow each student the opportunity to do one or more everyday activities that he or she enjoys as "free choice" stations during the allotted time.

- Develop a bulletin board entitled "Physical Activity—A 'Key' to a Healthy Lifestyle." Place a number of keys made of construction paper on the bulletin board, which lists a variety of physical activities. Place pictures of people (students or magazine and newspaper clippings) doing a variety of activities on the bulletin board. Examples of activities for keys include the following: washing and waxing a car, washing windows or floors, playing volleyball, playing touch football, gardening, wheeling self in a wheelchair, walking, playing basketball, bicycling, dancing, raking leaves, doing water aerobics, running fast, jogging, and shoveling snow.

SAMPLE INCLUSION TIP

Adaptations must be specific to the activities chosen. For example, for basketball shooting, set up baskets of several heights for students to choose from by using a hang-a-hoop basket, freestanding baskets, or adjustable baskets. Alter ball size, weight, and texture as needed.

ASSESSMENT

- Discuss the station recording charts. Discuss intensity in relation to body composition—higher-intensity activities burn more calories per minute, but people cannot maintain them as long as they can moderate activity. Discuss whether students listed an activity as aerobic or muscular (some do both!), and how both components of fitness contribute to body composition.

- Have students keep track of their activities for a week. They should mark the activities as moderate or vigorous and muscular or aerobic, and list the amount of time they spent on activity each day. Do they meet the recommendation for 60 minutes or more on most days of the week?

6.5 Little Bird Growing Dance

PRIMARY LEVEL

Growth and development—Physical activity and balanced nutrition contribute to a child's proper growth, and development of a healthy body composition.

PURPOSE

Children will learn that it is fun and healthy to participate in creative dance. They will relate the need for healthy food to growth and development of themselves and of animals.

RELATIONSHIP TO NATIONAL STANDARDS

National Dance Standard 6: The student will make connections between dance and healthful living.

Physical Education Standard 4: The student achieves and maintains a health-enhancing level of physical fitness.

EQUIPMENT

- Scarves (optional)
- Musical accompaniment (CDs or live, ideally with nature sounds)

Reproducible

None

PROCEDURE

1. Review the reasons for eating well and being physically active. Use birds as examples. To fly as many miles as they do, birds must eat the right foods and exercise their bodies. Ask the children what kinds of foods they need to eat so that they can dance or do another exercise. If you wish, give the children two scarves to hold in their hands, which can act as extensions to their wings (arms).

2. Read students a poem about birds. For example, read this poem:

   In the spring, as you know,

   Birds do grow and grow,

   They flap their wings and fly so high,

   And eat good foods as they crow,

   Now children, reach for the sky, oh my,

   For when you eat and exercise,

   You too will grow and grow

   From your head to your toes!

3. Have the students perform a warm-up.

   - Have the children sit on the floor and pretend that they are birds in their shells. They sit in imaginary nests that will serve as their personal spaces.

   - They will assume what is called the child pose in yoga. Sitting on their knees and curled forward, they pretend to use their beaks to break out of their shells.

- They slowly grow upward, reaching for the sky and using their arms like wings. Their arm movements may lead to jumps that they can count.
- If you wish, encourage the children to make birdlike sounds
- Discuss with the children how the mother bird first feeds the baby birds, and how the baby birds begin to seek out their own food.

© Human Kinetics

4. Have children step out of their nests and begin looking for worms (food).
   - They may use their feet like claws, and their faces like beaks.
   - Have the children demonstrate hops, jumps, turns, and balances on one leg as they begin to travel across the floor
5. Have the children move across the floor until they are told to go back to their nests.
6. Back in their nests, have the children perform a cool-down.
   - As they do this, they should slow their movements and contain them to their nests.
   - They eventually sit in their spaces.

TEACHING HINTS

■ Although this activity is about birds, you can easily use other animals, from snakes to frogs to butterflies! You may expand the idea of nature by having children move as water, a rainbow, or flowers. Add the metaphor of flowers growing and needing the rain and sun.

■ At this young age, children are learning to cooperate. Remind them in a pleasant way about respecting each other's space.

SAMPLE INCLUSION TIP

Students who are unable to hop, jump, turn, or balance on one leg, can perform their own body movements. Use different pathways, at different levels.

ASSESSMENT

Discuss with the children what they need to do to grow and be healthy (be active, eat a variety of nutritious foods). Have them name some activities and foods.

6.6   Nutrition Hunt

PRIMARY LEVEL

Nutrition—Through this activity and with the use of a Food Guide Pyramid, students learn about a balanced diet.

PURPOSE

Students will participate in collecting fruits, vegetables, and other foods to identify the food groups on the Food Guide Pyramid that contribute to a balanced diet.

RELATIONSHIP TO NATIONAL STANDARDS

Physical Education Standard 5: The student exhibits responsible personal and social behavior that respects self and others in physical activity settings.

Health Education Standard 1: The student will comprehend concepts related to health promotion and disease prevention.

EQUIPMENT

Poly spots

PROCEDURE

1. Prior to the day of the activity, assign students to cut out and bring in pictures they find that match up with the Food Guide Pyramid. You can assign students to bring in a sampling of pictures from all groupings on the pyramid, or divide the class and assign students to different food groups. You may also want to have them paste their pictures onto cardboard or index cards.

2. In class, collect the pictures and scatter them upside down in the middle of the activity space.

3. Explain the Food Guide Pyramid to the students, using a large poster of the pyramid, or the Food Guide Pyramid handouts as a visual aid. Have students offer examples for each grouping on the pyramid.

4. Divide students into small teams of approximately two to three students per group, and give each team one pencil and one Food Guide Pyramid handout, showing the photos and number of servings for each section of the pyramid.

5. Place groups around the perimeter of the activity space, with a poly spot or some other marker as each group's home base.

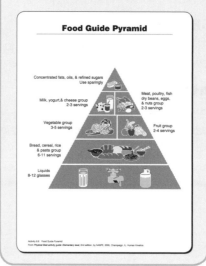

Reproducible

- Food Guide Pyramid to introduce lesson (make a copy for each student or pair of students)

6. On the "Go" signal, one student from each group should run out and pick up a food picture, bring it back and the team should determine where to check it off on their pyramid, placing a check next to the food group on the pyramid.

7. The students continue to run out to the pictures, taking turns, and as a group check off the pyramid until they fill one serving from each category. If the student brings back a card for a category that is already full, they should hand it to the next student to go out so that they can return it to the pile and bring back a new card.

© Human Kinetics

TEACHING HINTS

■ For younger students, ask them to simply pick up a food card, run it back, and then pick up another. As a class, put the foods into the food pyramid.

■ Have extra food pictures made ahead of time to supplement those brought in by the class.

SAMPLE INCLUSION TIP

When a student with a disability (crutches, wheelchair, visual impairment, and so on) goes to collect a food picture, other students must walk heel to toe.

ASSESSMENT

■ Check the food pyramids and pictures to see if the foods matched up correctly with the groupings on the Food Guide Pyramid.

■ Discuss what each team found for each grouping on the pyramid, and explain the number of servings of that grouping that they should have each day, and the variety of foods that fit in that grouping. Also, discuss the fats, oils, and refined sugars portion of the pyramid that does not have serving amounts. Explain that it is okay to have a small amount of foods from this category and that they are not forbidden, but that the students should not have too much of these types of foods causing them to have a "top heavy" or "exploding" pyramid.

6.7 Menu Maker

INTERMEDIATE LEVEL

Nutrition—A variety of foods from each food group on the Food Guide Pyramid provides the nutrients such as fat, carbohydrates, and proteins that people need for appropriate nutrition and a healthy body composition.

PURPOSE

Students will work cooperatively to create a day's menu and match it up to the Food Guide Pyramid to learn about a balanced and healthy diet.

RELATIONSHIP TO NATIONAL STANDARDS

Physical Education Standard 5: The student exhibits responsible personal and social behavior that respects self and others in physical activity settings.

Health Education Standard 1: The student will comprehend concepts related to health promotion and disease prevention.

EQUIPMENT

- Three hula hoops
- Poly spots
- Scooters
- Food pictures (see Procedure)

PROCEDURE

1. Prior to the day of the activity, assign students to cut out and bring in pictures they find that match up with the Food Guide Pyramid. You can assign students to bring in a sampling of pictures from all groupings on the pyramid, or divide the class and assign students to different food groups. You may also want to have them paste their pictures onto cardboard or index cards.

Reproducibles

- Food Guide Pyramid Worksheet
- Menu Maker Worksheet

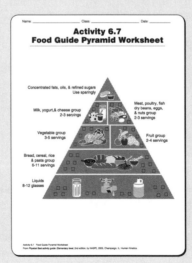

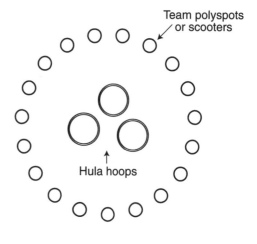

Team polyspots or scooters

Hula hoops

2. In class, collect the food group pictures and place them upside down in three hula hoops placed in the center of the activity space. Review the Food Guide Pyramid and provide examples for a serving size from each group.

3. Divide students into small teams of two to three students per team, and give each group a Menu Maker Worksheet and pencil.

4. Assign each team to a poly spot and scooter, spaced in a circle around the perimeter of the activity space.

5. On the "Go" signal, one student from each team rides the scooter out to one of the three hoops in the center of the activity space, picks up a food picture, and rides the scooter back to their team. The team members decide where the food fits on their menu, writes it in the appropriate space, and the next student then rides out to pick up a food picture.

6. Continue until students have picked up enough cards to fill a day's menu. Once completed, hand out a Food Guide Pyramid, and have students check off their menu items against the pyramid, to see if their foods ended up filling the pyramid correctly (at least the minimum and no more than the maximum servings per food group).

TEACHING HINTS

■ Have extra food pictures made ahead of time to supplement those brought in by the class.

■ Discuss food pictures that have multiple food groups represented, and how to check them off against their list. For example: a sandwich might have two pieces of breads (two servings of the bread, cereal, rice, and pasta group) as well as a piece of cheese (one serving from the milk, yogurt, and cheese group), and so on.

■ Copy enough Menu Maker Worksheets to have one for each student, have them fill in all of the sheets so that each student has a copy of the day's menu, and then have students complete the Food Guide Pyramid individually as a homework assignment.

■ Unsafe scooter drivers may have their license taken away.

■ As a variation, have seven hoops and put cards for a different food group in each hoop, and have students build a menu that fits the Food Guide Pyramid.

SAMPLE INCLUSION TIP

Place students who have difficulty reading into groups that will help them complete the pyramid task.

ASSESSMENT

■ Discuss the Food Guide Pyramid Worksheets. Did they meet the minimum number of servings for each food group, and not exceed the maximum number of servings? Discuss the role of chance and relate that to their eating habits (if they leave it to chance and do not consider their food choices, their pyramid may not be balanced).

■ Discuss what the teams did with the fats, oils, and refined sugars pictures. (They can keep a small amount. The Food Guide Pyramid does not forbid these foods, but people should not have too many and have a "top heavy" or "exploding" pyramid.)

■ Explain that the pyramid does not need to be "perfect" every day, but that over time they should be taking in the recommended servings from each group. Relate food choices over the long-term to effects on body composition.

6.8 Calorie Burn-Up

PRIMARY LEVEL

The way the body processes food into fuel is called **metabolism.** People with faster metabolisms burn calories faster than do those with slower metabolisms. The rate of metabolism affects body composition.

PURPOSE

Students will understand that although everyone needs the same nutrients, no two people have the same metabolism.

RELATIONSHIP TO NATIONAL STANDARDS

Physical Education Standard 4: The student achieves and maintains a health-enhancing level of physical fitness.

Health Education Standard 1: The student will comprehend concepts related to health promotion and disease prevention.

EQUIPMENT

- Beanbags, yarn balls, Nerf balls, or any other soft balls
- Crates or other targets
- Spots

Reproducible

None

PROCEDURE

1. Place students on the long side of the volleyball court in pairs (if a large class) or individually (if a small class) or create a similar activity space using tape or cones. Put the beanbags or balls out behind the students in a location that is easy to reach. Place crates or targets of your choice on the opposite volleyball court line.
2. On the "Go" signal, students throw a beanbag or ball toward a crate or target.
3. Make or miss, the students go to get another beanbag or ball, but they must walk to pick up the new object and walk back to their throwing spot.
4. Give the students 30 to 60 seconds (choose your time depending on class size and the time you have them in class). Then stop, empty the crates, pick up loose balls or beanbags, and get ready for Round 2.
5. Move the spot for throwing one-quarter of the way closer to the target.
6. Make or miss, the students go to get another beanbag or ball, but they must side slide to pick up the new object and side-slide back to their throwing spot.
7. Give the students 30 to 60 seconds. Then stop, empty the crates, pick up loose balls or beanbags, and get ready for Round 3.
8. Again, move the spot for throwing one-quarter of the way closer to the target.
9. Make or miss, the students go to get another beanbag or ball, but they must skip to pick up the new object and skip back to their throwing spot.

10. Give the students 30 to 60 seconds. Then stop, empty the crates, pick up loose balls or beanbags, and get ready for Round 4.

11. Again, move the spot for throwing one-quarter of the way closer to the target.

12. Make or miss, the students go to get another beanbag or ball, but they must run to pick up the new object and run back to their throwing spot.

13. Connect the activity to the lesson on metabolism by saying the following: The metabolism of some people uses food slowly, and more time is needed to use it up, like when we walked to pick up new beanbags or balls which were farther away. The metabolism of some people uses food more quickly, and less time is needed to use it up, like when we ran to pick up new balls or beanbags that were closer to us. Both the closer target and the faster locomotors represented the faster metabolism.

© Human Kinetics

TEACHING HINTS

■ Use the same time throughout the activity for each throwing distance.

■ Use shorter time when you have more students, short class time, and limited equipment.

■ You can do the same activity with kicking, striking with floor hockey sticks, and so on.

SAMPLE INCLUSION TIP

Alter the target (hoops, bowling pins), target location (on a table or chair), and allow other modifications (pushing instead of throwing objects) as needed to accomodate students with disabilities.

ASSESSMENT

■ Say, "The way the body processes food into fuel is called metabolism. Thumbs up if you agree, thumbs down if you disagree." (Answer: thumbs up.)

■ Ask, "Does everyone have the same metabolism? Thumbs up if you agree, thumbs down if you disagree." (Answer: thumbs down.)

■ Using the letters of the word *metabolism,* ask the classroom teacher to help the students place a body composition component or influencing-factor word for each letter, as in this example:

M = muscles

E = energy

T = target weight

A = activity

B = body fat

O = overweight or underweight

L = lean body mass

I = individual

S = society

M = moderation

6.9 Metabolism Medley

INTERMEDIATE LEVEL

The way the body processes food into fuel is called **metabolism.** People with faster metabolisms burn calories faster than do those with slower metabolisms. The rate of metabolism affects body composition.

PURPOSE

▪ Students will use the Physical Activity Pyramid for Children (Corbin 2004; CD-ROM) to learn how participating in a variety of physical activities helps people raise their metabolism and achieve and maintain healthy body composition.

▪ Students will participate in a variety of physical activities to help them raise their metabolism, and achieve and maintain a healthy body composition.

RELATIONSHIP TO NATIONAL STANDARDS

Physical Education Standard 4: The student achieves and maintains a health-enhancing level of physical fitness.

Health Education Standard 1: The student will comprehend concepts related to health promotion and disease prevention.

EQUIPMENT

▪ Equipment as needed for enough muscular strength and endurance, flexibility, and aerobic fitness stations to keep groups small (4-6 students) (please see activities in chapters 3, 4, and 5 for ideas)

▪ Upbeat music and music player

PROCEDURE

1. Tell or ask students what the word *metabolism* means related to body composition. Explain that, while metabolism is partly due to your individual makeup (and this part cannot be changed), part of your metabolism can be changed. Physical activity can help increase metabolism in all people.

• *Aerobic fitness* activities burn calories, increasing metabolism.

• Muscle cells burn (metabolize) more calories at rest than fat cells do. Having good *muscular strength and endurance* may help increase metabolism.

• Good *flexibility* helps keep you more active overall. A flexible body helps

Reproducible

▪ 1 photocopy of the Physical Activity Pyramid for Children per student and 1 Physical Activity Pyramid for Children poster for display (the poster is optional—call Human Kinetics at 800-747-4457 for ordering information)

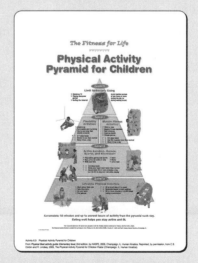

Reprinted, by permission, from C. Corbin and R. Lindsey, 2004, *Fitness for Life*, 5th ed. (Champaign, IL: Human Kinetics).

you perform aerobic fitness and muscular strength and endurance activities better and more safely.

2. Introduce or review the Physical Activity Pyramid for Children. Point out how a variety of everyday, recreation, and sport activities help meet everyone's needs and interests while working on good body composition.

3. Send students in small groups through the stations.

TEACHING HINTS

■ Make the connection between the word *metamorphosis*, which students may be more familiar with, and metabolism. For example, a caterpillar or tadpole metamorphose, or *change*, into a butterfly or frog. We can *change* our metabolism through participating regularly in a variety of physical activities.

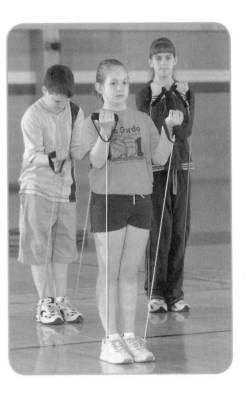

■ When revisiting this activity, vary the station activities to best meet your current skill unit while addressing each component of health-related fitness.

■ Extend the lesson to tie nutrition into metabolism:

• Explain that the body is a Calorie Machine, and if more calories go in than out (long term), it can lead to less healthy body composition.

• Remind students how physical activity can help increase metabolism, or the body's burning of calories.

• As homework, give students one week to design a Calorie Machine Diagram, drawing a gadget that shows a list of foods eaten during the a day going into a machine. Have students draw a variety of physical activity choices that send calories out.

• Have a few students share their Calorie Machines each class time until all have had a chance.

SAMPLE INCLUSION TIP

Modify the stations selected for the activity to provide for students with disabilities.

ASSESSMENT

■ Ask, "Which components of health-related fitness can you participate in to improve or keep a healthy body composition?"

■ Look for application of the concept: As homework over the next week, require students to mark each activity they participate in on their photocopy of the Physical Activity Pyramid for Children. Encourage them to write in additional activity types not listed in the correct areas of the pyramid.

CHAPTER

7

Special Events

Chapter Contents

- Activities

PhotoDisc

Students are more likely to participate in physical activity if they have opportunities to develop interests that are personally meaningful to them. The developmentally appropriate activities included in this chapter provide students with fun and meaningful activities while celebrating holidays, traditions, and special health and physical education observances. The previous chapters center on teaching the health-related fitness concepts and principles through a variety of activities focused on the components of health-related fitness. The activities in this chapter connect what students do in physical education class with their lives outside physical education. Both are important to the development of an active, healthy lifestyle.

These activities also use several of the multiple intelligence strategies that we have come to know and use in quality physical education programs (Gardner 1993). Multiple intelligence theory is concerned with the process of learning. Students learn in many different ways, and in fitness development, "variety is the spice of life." What students do, they understand!

In keeping with the Physical Best program philosophy, the activities in this chapter teach fitness concepts through bodily-kinesthetic intelligence while integrating the remaining intelligences (musical, linguistic, intrapersonal, interpersonal, logical-mathematical, and spatial) into the lessons and extensions of the lessons to increase opportunities for success for all students.

Many health-related organizations keep updated lists of National Health Observances, which can generate additional fun and educational activity ideas for students. One such resource is the U.S. Department of Health and Human Services "healthfinder" Web site. To access the healthfinder National Health Observances calendar, go to www.healthfinder.gov/library/nho/.

In addition to the special events activities found in this chapter, you'll find a reproducible on the CD-ROM called the ABCs of Fitness. The alphabet is a building block for learning to read and write. Use the fitness ABCs as a building block in physical education class, too. Each letter of the alphabet corresponds with a concept included in the Physical Best and FITNESSGRAM programs. The alphabet can be used to reinforce the concepts and principles taught during the daily fitness development activity, or at the end of the lesson as part of a closure activity. Week by week, let Physical Best help students reach their peak.

Activities

Chapter 7 Activities Grid

Activity number	Activity title	Activity page	Concept	Primary	Intermediate	Month	Reproducible (on CD-ROM)
7.1	Mind Map Health-Related Fitness Circuit	155	Identifying fitness components; circuit training for FITNESS-GRAM assessments, conditioning activities		●	September	Mind Map Station Signs (each includes definitions, FITNESSGRAM assessments and free choice conditioning activities)
7.2	Fall Into Fitness Circuit	158	Identifying fitness components	●		October	Fall Into Fitness Circuit Signs
7.3	Harvest Exercise Hunt	160	Circuit training for fitness options		●	October-November	Harvest Hunt Task Cards
7.4	Thanksgiving Benefits Circuit	162	Benefits of fitness		●	November	Thanksgiving Benefits Circuit Station Signs
							Family Homework Assignment—Benefits of Fitness
7.5	The 12 Days of Fitness	165	Fitness components	●	●	December	12 Days of Fitness Task Cards
							12 Days of Fitness Family Activity Sheet
7.6	Physical Best Crossword Puzzle	168	Concept knowledge assessment		●	January	Physical Best Crossword Puzzle
7.7	Healthy Heart Exercise Hunt	170	Specificity of training for aerobic fitness (Type)		●	February	Healthy Heart Exercise Hunt Task Cards
7.8	Heart Smart Orienteering	172	Aerobic fitness and FITT; benefits of activity; warning signs for heart disease and stroke; cooperative learning		●	February	Orienteering Master Sheet
							Heart Smart Orienteering Questions
							FITT Homework Assignment
7.9	Everyday and Sometimes Foods	175	Nutrition and food choices using the food pyramid		●	March	Everyday and Sometimes Food Assessment
							Treat Challenge Sheets
7.10	Spring Into Fitness	178	Total fitness circuit; benefits of activity and risks associated with inactivity		●	April	Spring Into Fitness Task Cards

(continued)

Activity number	Activity title	Activity page	Concept	Primary	Intermediate	Month	Reproducible (on CD-ROM)
7.11	Project ACES	180	Cooperative learning; activity celebration	●	●	May	Exercise Hunt Task Cards
7.12	Catch the Thrill of the Skill	182	HRF and SRF circuit motor-skill themes integration		●	May	Health-Related and Skill-Related Fitness Station Signs
7.13	Dash for Cash	185	HR Fitness components; activity celebration	●	●	May or June	Dash for Cash Fitness Station Signs
7.14	Summer Fun— Summer Shape-Up Challenge	188	Benefits of activity and risks of inactivity	●	●	June, July, or August	Summer Shape-Up Challenge Activity Sheet

7.1 Mind Map Health-Related Fitness Circuit

INTERMEDIATE LEVEL

September—Identifying fitness components; circuit training for *FITNESSGRAM* assessments; and conditioning activities.

PURPOSE

The first four steps outlined in the Fitness Education Process for the Physical Best and *FITNESSGRAM* programs (see *FITNESSGRAM/ACTIVITYGRAM Test Administration Manual, Third Edition,* pages 12-13) include instruction about fitness concepts, student participation in conditioning activities, instruction on test items, and assessment of fitness levels. The Mind Map Health-Related Fitness Circuit includes all four steps and integrates both the knowledge of the five health-related fitness components with the critical elements of the accompanying *FITNESSGRAM* assessments into one lesson. Students will identify and define the five health-related fitness components, learn the names and critical elements of the accompanying *FITNESSGRAM* assessments, participate in the assessments, and select one or two personally meaningful conditioning activities that will help them achieve and maintain a health-enhancing level of fitness.

RELATIONSHIP TO NATIONAL STANDARDS

Physical Education Standard 3: The student participates regularly in physical activity.

Physical Education Standard 4: The student achieves and maintains a health-enhancing level of physical fitness.

Health Education Standard 1: The student will comprehend concepts related to health promotion and disease prevention.

EQUIPMENT

- 45-30 segmented music tape (45 seconds of music, 30 seconds of rest) and player
- 10 cones
- Tumbling mats or carpet squares
- Curl-up strips
- Trunk lift rulers
- Two to four hula hoops
- Beanbags

If you use the free choice activities listed on the CD-ROM reproducible, you will need additional equipment—jump ropes, balls, resistive exercise bands, and so on.

Reproducible

- Mind Map Station Signs—Mind Map definitions for the five health-related fitness components, plus free choice conditioning activities and accompanying *FITNESSGRAM* assessments

Aerobic Fitness

The ability of the heart and lungs to supply oxygen to the working muscles for an extended period of time.

 Mind Map
. . . heart, lungs, and muscles working overtime!

Having good aerobic fitness allows you to enjoy moderate and vigorous activity over time!

Activity 7.1 Mind Map Station Signs
From *Physical Best activity guide: Elementary level*, 2nd edition, by NASPE, 2005, Champaign, IL: Human Kinetics.

PROCEDURE

Week 1

1. Set up the circuit by placing the Mind Map Station Signs (definitions) and assessment signs at each station.

2. Demonstrate the critical elements for each of the assessments.

3. Divide the class up equally among the stations, or use squads.

4. Use the segmented music tape (45-30).

5. Students perform the assessment activities while the music plays. When the music stops, students clean up and then rotate to the next station. While resting and waiting for the music to begin again, students read the Mind Map definition on the new fitness station sign. When the music begins, resume activity. Repeat the sequence until students have completed all five stations.

Week 2

Monitor and adjust the activity based on the knowledge and age of your students. Third graders may need to practice the assessments again, whereas fifth graders may be ready to participate in the free choice activities at each station.

© Human Kinetics

TEACHING HINTS

▨ Because the body composition assessment in *FITNESSGRAM* is a skinfold measurement or body mass index, we included the Physical Best activity "What's the Mix?" (Activity 6.2, page 134) in the circuit, which teaches the definition of body composition. You can change this or add a novel activity that your students enjoy (practicing their favorite aerobic sport skill; moving, tossing, and catching with a piece of equipment; climbing a rock wall, and so on).

▨ Use tumbling mats or carpet squares at both the muscular endurance (curl-up) and flexibility (trunk lift) stations. Place the curl-up strips and the trunk lift rulers at these stations as visual aids.

- Use pictures on station signs to demonstrate critical elements to help younger students who may still be nonreaders.
- Plan a family fitness night and invite parents to learn about your Physical Best/ *FITNESSGRAM* Program. Use the Mind Map Health-Related Fitness Circuit as your fitness activity for the night. Make sure parents understand that health-related fitness standards are criterion referenced, based on a criterion to be healthy, and that they do not compare student with student. Our goal is to help all children become their physical best: Encourage all students, challenge the athlete, and include those with special needs!

SAMPLE INCLUSION TIPS

- Have a peer tutor use a wand or baton to help a student who is blind participate in the PACER activity.
- At the curl-up station, students with special needs will need assistance (holding feet or holding on to partner's fingers).

ASSESSMENT

- Have students define one or more of the five health-related fitness components using the Mind Maps as a guide. For example, aerobic endurance is the ability of the _____ and _____ to supply _____ to the working muscles over time.
- Have students name the *FITNESSGRAM* assessment for each component of fitness. Can they name at least two critical elements for each assessment?
- Have students work in small groups to list two or three new activities to include at each of the fitness stations for personal and free choice conditioning activities in week 2 for this activity.

7.2   Fall Into Fitness Circuit

PRIMARY LEVEL

October—Identifying fitness components.

PURPOSE

As the weather starts to change and fall approaches, students in most parts of the country have some new options for enjoying physical activity both indoors and outdoors. In this activity, students will participate in a fun health-related fitness circuit training activity that promotes and encourages group cooperation. Students will understand that a healthy heart and strong muscles allow them to participate in a variety of physical activities.

RELATIONSHIP TO NATIONAL STANDARDS

Physical Education Standard 3: The student participates regularly in physical activity.

EQUIPMENT

- Segmented music tape (40 seconds of music, 15 seconds of rest) and player
- 10 to 12 large cones for station signs
- Six to eight small cones for scooter station
- Tumbling mats
- Specialty equipment for the Wellness Corner (jump ropes, resistance bands, and so on)

PROCEDURE

1. Use a fun fall song, such as "Itsy Bitsy Spider," to make a segmented (40-15) music tape with 40 seconds of music and 15 seconds of rest.
2. Set up the circuit as shown in diagram.
3. Place tumbling mats at the Curl-up challenge and Spider-web stations.
4. Demonstrate any new and novel activities to the students.
5. Students work in groups (squads).
6. Assign each squad a starting station.
7. When the music plays, students work at a station. When the music stops, students rotate to the next station. Continue until students have completed the circuit.

Reproducible

- Fall Into Fitness Circuit Signs

Jog Around the Pumpkin Patch

When you pass another group of students exercising, cheer them on and encourage them to keep working hard.

To rest is to rust!

Activity 7.2 · Fall Into Fitness Station Signs
From *Physical Best activity guide: Elementary level*, 2nd edition, by NASPE, 2005, Champaign, IL: Human Kinetics.

TEACHING HINTS

- Use some fun fall props to make the activity more enjoyable for students (leaves, skeleton for bones, pumpkins, spider web, and so on).

- To help the nonreader, use pictures to demonstrate each activity or exercise on your signs.

- Develop a bulletin board for October that says, "Treat your body right and it won't trick you!" We treat our bodies right when we eat a variety of foods from the food groups and choose to be active most days of the week.

- October includes Walk Your Child to School Day. Plan a way to promote walking as a great fall activity.

Visit the Centers for Disease Control (CDC) Web site at www.cdc.gov/nccdphp/dnpa/kidswalk.htm to learn more about this annual health promotion for kids and families.

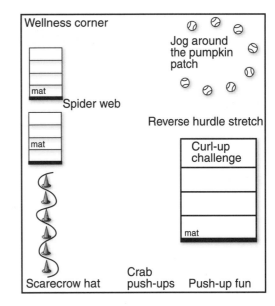

SAMPLE INCLUSION TIPS

- Help students with special needs focus on the critical aspects of the movement or fitness skills by giving them one- or two-word cues.

- Have older students serve as peer tutors to help younger students at each station (work this out ahead of time with classroom teachers).

- Use visual cues to change from station to station.

ASSESSMENT

- Ask students, "At what two stations did your heart beat the fastest? Why?"

- Ask students, "At what station did your arm muscles work the hardest?"

- Think-Pair-Share—Have students discuss with a friend their favorite activities in the circuit. Were they the same or different activities? Why or why not?

7.3   Harvest Exercise Hunt

INTERMEDIATE LEVEL

October-November—Circuit training for fitness options.

PURPOSE

- Students will participate in a fun, interpersonal, and cooperative learning fall fitness activity.
- Students will identify the muscular strength and endurance activities that help them develop good posture and strong, healthy muscles.

RELATIONSHIP TO NATIONAL STANDARDS

Physical Education Standard 4: The student achieves and maintains a health-enhancing level of fitness. The student identifies the components of health-related fitness.

EQUIPMENT

- Four to six poly spots or cones
- Four tumbling mats
- Props—pumpkins, spider web, hay bales, plastic fruit and veggies (apples, corn)
- Fall song (continuous) and player—some suggestions are "Itsy Bitsy Spider," "Monster Mash," and because this activity includes fruits and vegetables, Dole 5 A Day has a great cassette with lots of fun songs on it. Visit www.dole5aday.com for more information.

PROCEDURE

1. Demonstrate the novel activities to students. By "novel" we refer to new ideas not necessarily included in fitness activities so far this year, such as a crop circle, apple pass, and so on.
2. Students work in groups of four to six. They can work in squads, or you can let students choose their groups (whistle mixer). Each group will need a designated leader to get the activity started.
3. Determine a home base for each group. The home base could be a poly spot or cone where the group will keep their hunt card.
4. While the music plays, students participate in the activities in the order listed on their cards. All task cards include the same activities, but each card lists them in a different order. This activity involves continuous movement.

Reproducible

- Harvest Hunt Task Cards

Harvest Hunt

1. **CORN-ON-THE-COB RELAY.** Use the cob as a baton and jog as a group around the activity area two times while passing the baton from person to person. When the last person in the group gets the cob, he or she runs to the front and starts again. Cheer on other teams as you move around the gym.
2. **APPLE PASS.** Try 12 to 15 partner push-ups while passing the apple back and forth.
3. **TRACTOR PULL TO THE PUMPKIN PATCH.** Make a straight line with your team. Stay connected (hold waists or hands on the shoulders) and jog to one of the pumpkin signs. Jog around the sign once and then head to the next pumpkin. Repeat the pattern until you have jogged around all three pumpkins.
4. **JUICE STAND.** Get a drink. How many glasses of water should you drink in a day?
5. **HAY BALE.** Do three curl-up challenges at each of the hay bales in the four corners of the activity area.
6. **CROP CIRCLE.** Stand in a straight line holding hands with your group. Wrap up your group around one person and move as a group. Walk with small steps and touch the two end lines of the gym or activity area.
7. **CHARLOTTE'S WEB.** Crab walk to Charlotte's web and back.
8. **FALL INTO FITNESS.** Choose three of your favorite stretches and hold each one for 10 to 30 seconds.

Activity 7.3   Harvest Hunt Task Cards
From *Physical Best activity guide: Elementary level*, 2nd edition, by NASPE, 2005, Champaign, IL: Human Kinetics.

5. Students stay connected by hands or wrists while performing the activities.

6. The leader helps count or keep track of time as needed.

7. Students walk to cool down after performing the hunt. You may want to ask assessment questions during the cool-down phases of your fitness focus.

TEACHING HINTS

- No group of students should follow another group from station to station. Explain to the students that each task card has the same activities but that each group will do the activities in a different order.

- Place tumbling mats in the corners where students will perform curl-up activities.

- Challenge individual students to perform the push-up activity at the level of difficulty (intensity) that is best for them.

- To create a fall-like atmosphere, use a cornucopia and place the plastic fruit and veggies in it. Place some small hay bales in the corners (or use pictures).

SAMPLE INCLUSION TIP

Conduct activities on a smooth surface to allow students that use crutches, canes, wheelchairs, and the like the opportunity to travel safely.

ASSESSMENT

Ask students to identify the activities in the hunt that developed their muscular strength. Ask them which activities developed their muscular endurance. Which developed both muscular strength and muscular endurance? Have students name three benefits of having good muscular strength and endurance.

7.4 Thanksgiving Benefits Circuit

INTERMEDIATE LEVEL

November—Benefits of fitness.

PURPOSE

Thanksgiving is a great time for students and their families to be thankful for the many benefits they receive by choosing to develop and maintain active, healthy lifestyles. In this intrapersonal fitness activity, students work individually by rank ordering the health benefits included in the circuit according to individual importance, and they participate in fun physical activities espousing those benefits. Students will list three to five benefits of health-related fitness and how those benefits influence their lifestyle.

RELATIONSHIP TO NATIONAL STANDARDS

Physical Education Standard 3: The student participates regularly in physical activity.

Health Education Standard 1: The student will comprehend concepts related to health promotion and disease prevention. The student will describe how physical, social, and emotional environments influence personal health.

Health Education Standard 3: The student will demonstrate the ability to practice health-enhancing behaviors and reduce health risks. The student will identify personal health needs and apply skills to manage stress.

EQUIPMENT

- 45-45 segmented music tape (45 seconds of music, 45 seconds of rest) and player
- 8 to10 cones
- Two to four tumbling mats
- Long and short jump ropes
- Aerobic steps

Reproducibles

- Thanksgiving Benefits Circuit Station Signs
- Family Homework Assignment—Benefits of Fitness

More Enjoyment in Life

Choose your favorite physical activity to participate in!

Activity 7.4 Thanksgiving Benefits Circuit Station Signs
From *Physical Best activity guide: Elementary level*, 2nd edition, by NASPE, 2005, Champaign, IL: Human Kinetics.

Name: _____ Class: _____ Date: _____

Activity 7.4
Family Homework Assignment—Benefits of Fitness

People choose to exercise for many reasons. Leading a healthy, active lifestyle has many benefits, one of which is increased life expectancy (live longer)!

List your top five benefits of exercise you chose during our Thanksgiving Health Benefits Circuit in physical education class.

_____
_____
_____
_____
_____

What are some factors that may change your reasons for exercising as you get older?

_____
_____

Ask an adult to list his or her top five benefits of exercise here.

_____
_____
_____
_____
_____

Are your benefits of exercise different than the adults? Why or why not?

_____
_____

Activity 7.4 Family Homework Assignment—Benefits of Fitness
From *Physical Best activity guide: Elementary level*, 2nd edition, by NASPE, 2005, Champaign, IL: Human Kinetics.

- Jump bands
- Balls—soccer, basketball, football, and so on
- Hockey sticks and pucks
- Specialty equipment for your novel activities (circus events, juggling scarves, stationary bikes, rock wall, and so on) or your school favorites (two-square, four-square, and so on)

PROCEDURE

1. Find a fun, fast-paced song and make a 45-45 segmented music tape.
2. Set up the circuit using your activity area and any specialty equipment you will use (rock wall, circus events, stationary bikes, jump bands, long jump ropes, and so on) to maximize the learning experience for students.
3. Students warm up by walking around the activity area, looking at each benefit sign and beginning to rank order the benefits by their importance to them.
4. When students are ready to begin, they jog to the station that corresponds with their number 1 benefit choice (more enjoyment of life, sleep better, less stress, learn better, better at sports, and so forth) and raise their hands.
5. When the music begins, students work at the benefit station, performing the accompanying physical activity at that station. When the music stops, students clean up and then jog to their second most important benefit. Once there, they look at you and perform the stretch that you are doing until the music begins. The sequence continues until students have participated in six to eight of the benefit stations.

© Human Kinetics

TEACHING HINTS

- Use some activities that represent physical activities found in your region of the country (for example, pretend to cross-country ski or ride a bicycle).
- Students can be the leaders for the stretches performed after each physical activity.

- On the second day that students perform the circuit, challenge them to increase the intensity (how hard they work) at the health-related fitness stations.

- Create a bulletin board that says, "PE Brings good things to life." Include pictures (students from your school or graphics) and words espousing the many benefits included in this activity—look good, feel good, learn better, have more energy, have less stress, have stronger muscles, enjoy life more, be better at sports, and so on.

SAMPLE INCLUSION TIP

Let a student with special needs stay at the same station for two rotations to minimize transitions.

ASSESSMENT

Think-Pair-Share—Have students discuss their top three benefits with a partner. Were any of the benefits the same? Different? Why?

7.5

The 12 Days of Fitness

PRIMARY OR INTERMEDIATE LEVELS

December—Fitness components.

PURPOSE

The holidays are a magical time of year for American children. This fun physical activity is a take on a traditional holiday song. By varying the teaching style used (command or cooperative learning groups), the intensity of the activities, and the type of exercises included in the activity, you can use it with all grades. Students will identify one activity performed for each of the five health-related fitness components.

RELATIONSHIP TO NATIONAL STANDARDS

Physical Education Standard 3: The student participates regularly in physical activity.

EQUIPMENT

- Holiday or winter music tape for continuous music and player ("Jingle Bells" works great because there is no mention of a religious holiday in the song.)
- Wrapped present box
- Poly spots or cones (10-12)
- Playground balls
- Hula hoops

Reproducibles

- 12 Days of Fitness Task Cards (both primary and intermediate versions)
- 12 Days of Fitness Family Activity Sheet (to be completed during the winter break with family and friends)

❄❄
❄ **On the first day of fitness, my PE teacher gave to me . . .**

One minute of my favorite locomotor activity!

Jog, skip, jump, slide, and so on.

❄❄❄

Activity 7.5 12 Days of Fitness Task Cards (primary)
From *Physical Best activity guide: Elementary level,* 2nd edition, by NASPE, 2005, Champaign, IL: Human Kinetics.

❄
On the first day of fitness, my PE teacher gave to me . . .
❄
One minute of my favorite aerobic activity!

Jog or walk around the gym, jump rope, do step-ups, and so on.

❄

Activity 7.5 12 Days of Fitness Task Cards (intermediate)
From *Physical Best activity guide: Elementary level,* 2nd edition, by NASPE, 2005, Champaign, IL: Human Kinetics.

MERRY FITNESS AND A HAPPY NEW YOU!!!
Dear Students,

I have enjoyed working with you this fall in physical education class. Have a great winter break! The holidays are a busy time for you and your family. Many exciting things will be happening around your homes during the winter break. To keep physical education on your minds and to promote an active, healthy lifestyle for you and your families, my gift to you is this fun and fitness-filled holiday activity! Take some time each day to sing the song and try the activities listed to keep your heart, lungs, and muscles strong and healthy! Happy exercising!

∗∗∗∗∗ **THE 12 DAYS OF FITNESS** ∗∗∗∗∗

On the **FIRST** day of fitness, my PE teacher gave to me . . . a heart-healthy family! Plan a family walk to look at all the spectacular holiday lights in the community.
On the **SECOND** day of fitness, my PE teacher gave to me . . . Two minutes of my favorite sport-skill activity! Play catch, dribble a ball, shoot some baskets, jump rope, or do another activity that you enjoy.
On the **THIRD** day of fitness, my PE teacher gave to me . . . Three minutes of wonderful wall-sits! Hold each wall sit for 30 seconds; get your quadriceps in shape for ski season.
On the **FOURTH** day of fitness, my PE teacher gave to me . . . Four fantastic sets of push-up fun with my family! Hands go over, over, back , back across a line; try each set for 15 seconds.
On the **FIFTH** day of fitness, my PE teacher gave to me . . . Five minutes of my favorite aerobic activity! Walk, hike, jog, bike, jump rope, roller skates, or do another activity. Be safe and wear a helmet to bike or skate.
On the **SIXTH** day of fitness, my PE teacher gave to me . . . Six super stretches! Try the sit-and-reach. Hold each stretch for 10 to 30 seconds and alternate legs.
On the **SEVENTH** day of fitness, my PE teacher gave to me . . . Seven jolly jumping jacks! Have FUN getting fit!
On the **EIGHTH** day of fitness, my PE teacher gave to me . . . Eight awesome arm circles! Try eight sets—forward and backward, big and small; work those deltoids.
On the **NINTH** day of fitness, my PE teacher gave to me . . . Nine hearty laughs! I hope that you are enjoying your winter break with family and friends.
On the **TENTH** day of fitness, my PE teacher gave to me . . . Ten minutes of my favorite aerobic sport activity! Jump rope or play basketball, soccer, hockey, or play another sport.
On the **ELEVENTH** day of fitness, my PE teacher gave to me . . . Eleven courageous curl-ups! Hold each curl-up for four seconds up and two seconds down; work those abdominal muscles.
On the **TWELFTH** day of fitness, my PE teacher gave to me . . . a heart-healthy family! Plan a special activity to promote physical activity, fitness, and fun for the whole family.

Enjoy a healthy and happy holiday season! See you in January!
—Physical Education Teacher

Activity 7.5 12 Days of Fitness Family Activity Sheet
From *Physical Best activity guide: Elementary level,* 2nd edition, by NASPE, 2005, Champaign, IL: Human Kinetics.

■ Aerobic steps or folded mats

■ Jump ropes

■ Specialty equipment (jump bands, steps, juggling scarves, rock wall, and so on)

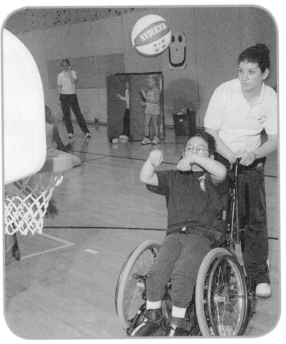

© Human Kinetics

PROCEDURE

For intermediate grades (grades 3 to 5):

1. Place the fitness signs inside the present box.

2. Place the equipment needed to participate in the activity around the perimeter of your activity area.

3. Students work with three or four friends in small groups, allowing for better on-task behavior close to the winter break.

4. Each group designates a team leader. The leader jogs to the present box picks up one of the 12 activity signs, brings it back to the group, and reads the sign. All students in the group perform the designated activity.

5. When the group finishes the first activity, the leader chooses another student to return the sign and pick out a new sign. The sequence repeats itself until everyone in the group has had at least two turns to pick out a sign and lead the group or until the designated fitness development activity time ends.

For primary grades (K through 2):

1. Students will work with the teacher to perform the activity.

2. Work right through the 12 Days of Fitness activity beginning with day 1: "On the first day of fitness, my PE teacher gave to me . . . one minute of my favorite locomotor activity!"

TEACHING HINTS

■ Explain any of the novel ideas included in the activities (wall push-ups, push-up fun, and so on).

■ With primary students, you lead (command style) but could have a different student helper read each number and help lead the class.

■ With intermediate grades, groups should spread out around the perimeter of the activity area, and each group should have a designated spot, a home base to work from (poly spots or cones work well).

■ For an extra challenge, make the groups stay connected (by hands or wrists) when the activity requires them to move around the activity space.

■ Create some fun holiday bulletin boards like these: "'Tis the Season to Be Healthy," "Merry Fitness and a Happy New You!!!" and "Light Up Your Life With Daily Physical Activity!"

SAMPLE INCLUSION TIPS

- The tasks on the cards may need to be modified for students with special needs. For example, you may want to reduce the number of repetitions, do wall push-ups rather than regular push-ups, and so on.
- A student with a visual impairment could use a hula hoop that makes noise.

ASSESSMENT

- Ask students to name at least one activity they performed that helped them improve their aerobic fitness. Ask the same question about flexibility, muscular endurance, and muscular strength.
- Ask students to complete this statement: To maintain a healthy body composition, you should _____ and _____.

7.6 Physical Best Crossword Puzzle

INTERMEDIATE LEVEL

January—Concept knowledge assessment.

PURPOSE

How are you doing in your quest to become your physical best? January is the month when many adults set New Year's resolutions. People vow to get in shape, exercise more, cut down on sweets, watch less TV, and so on. This month our activity is a knowledge assessment, a check-up to see if students are learning the Physical Best–*FITNESSGRAM* concepts that you have included in your health-related physical education program this year. Students will set at least one personal health-related fitness goal because of what they have learned. We know that students and families who have acquired the knowledge, skills, appreciation, and confidence needed to lead healthy and physically active lives are more apt to set New Year's goals related to fitness and physical activity. What we truly value, we do!

RELATIONSHIP TO NATIONAL STANDARDS

Physical Education Standard 3: The student participates regularly in physical activity.

Physical Education Standard 4: The student achieves and maintains a health-enhancing level of physical fitness.

Health Education Standard 6: The student will demonstrate the ability to use goal-setting and decision-making skills to enhance health.

EQUIPMENT

Pencils

PROCEDURE

1. Make copies of the Physical Best Crossword Puzzle.

2. You can administer the puzzle in several ways, depending on what you wish to accomplish with it.

   • Have students fill out the puzzle to the best of their ability as you return from the winter break.

   • Take one day to fill out the across answers; take another day to fill out the down answers.

   • Work together as a class. Help students fill out the puzzle by letting those who know the answers share them with their classmates.

Reproducible

■ Physical Best Crossword Puzzle

PHYSICAL BEST CROSSWORD PUZZLE

Across

5. Strong abdominal muscles help you maintain good _____.
6. The "bulb" muscle in your arms. Clue: rhymes with triceps!
7. The _____-_____-_____ assessment measures your flexibility in the lower back and hamstrings.
8. _____ means to "do a little more" each time you exercise.
13. _____ means to "work harder" each time your exercise.
15. _____ is the FITT principle that explains the number of days per week you should exercise.
16. Your _____ is the muscle that works like a pump.
17. _____ is the FITT principle that tells you the number of minutes you should exercise aerobically each day.
18. _____ fitness is the ability to work and play with energy to spare. Clue: Let's get _____! (an old song)

Down

1. Skinfold _____ are used to measure your skinfold thickness.
2. _____ fitness is the ability of the heart, lungs, and muscles to use oxygen efficiently over an extended time.
3. Muscular _____ is the ability to exert force to a muscle.
4. How hard you work is called _____.
6. _____ can be defined as the ratio of lean muscle mass to fat.
8. The _____ is the *FITNESSGRAM* assessment that measures your aerobic fitness.
9. Exercise makes muscles become _____. Clue: rhymes with longer!
10. A benefit of aerobic fitness. Clue: you can play longer.
11. To maintain a healthy body composition, eat a _____ _____ (two words) and follow a regular program of exercise or activity.
12. Foods that give your muscles energy to move are _____.
14. _____ strength and endurance are two of the five health-related fitness components.

Activity 7.6 Physical Best Crossword Puzzle
From *Physical Best activity guide: Elementary level*, 2nd edition, by NASPE, 2005, Champaign, IL: Human Kinetics.

TEACHING HINTS

- Give students clues to some of the harder questions. (See samples already built in to the puzzle.)

- Blow up a copy of the puzzle and place it on a bulletin board close to your exit door. Use the questions as a check for understanding for closure throughout the month.

- Create a "New Year's Resolution" bulletin board. Have students place their New Year's health and fitness goals on it.

SAMPLE INCLUSION TIPS

- A student with special needs could work with a peer helper to answer the questions.

- Verbal prompts might help a student understand the questions better.

ASSESSMENT

- The puzzle is an assessment. Students could work with partners to correct papers and check answers.

- Ask students, "Was there a question in the puzzle that you found very hard to answer?"

7.7 Healthy Heart Exercise Hunt

INTERMEDIATE LEVEL

February—Specificity of training for aerobic fitness (type).

PURPOSE

The American Heart Association sponsors Heart Month each February. The intent of this national celebration is to educate Americans about cardiovascular disease and to promote the benefits of living an active, healthy lifestyle. In this activity, students participate in a cooperative learning fitness activity that reinforces the concept of specificity of training (type) for aerobic fitness. Students will name three activities in the hunt that were continuous, used the large muscle groups, and improved their aerobic fitness.

RELATIONSHIP TO NATIONAL STANDARDS

Physical Education Standard 4: The student achieves and maintains a health-enhancing level of physical fitness.

Health Education Standard 3: The student will demonstrate the ability to practice health-enhancing behaviors and reduce health risks.

EQUIPMENT

- Music tape and player
- Six poly spots or cones

PROCEDURE

1. Place the Healthy Heart Exercise Hunt Task Cards on cones around the perimeter of the activity area, or under poly spots.

2. Explain and demonstrate any new or novel activities included on the hunt cards.

3. Students work in groups of four to six or in squads. Designate a leader to be in charge at each group. The leader keeps track of repetitions and keeps the group on task.

4. Play a fun heart song during the activity. Suggestion: "Every Heartbeat."

5. Students perform the activities on their hunt cards in the order in which they are listed. They will work continuously while the music plays.

6. An exercise hunt allows all students in the class to participate in the same physical activities, but each group performs them in a different order.

Reproducible

- Healthy Heart Exercise Hunt Task Cards

Your team must stay connected when performing all aerobic activities!

1. Skip around the gym or activity area two times.
2. Try 10 wall push-ups with a partner.
3. Try the human clock 3 times.
4. Do the back-saver sit-and-reach for 20 seconds on each leg.
5. Touch 4 boundary lines or 4 walls while you jog.
6. Push-up fun with a partner. Spell your favorite aerobic activity while in the push-up position.
7. Tag 5 people wearing red.
8. Stand up and sit down 3 times. (Work together!)

Aerobic Fitness is the ability of the heart and lungs to supply oxygen to the working muscles for an extended period of time.

Work as a TEAM . . . **Together Everyone Achieves More!!!**

Activity 7.7 Healthy Heart Exercise Hunt Task Cards.
From Physical Best activity guide: Elementary level, 2nd edition, by NASPE, 2005, Champaign, IL: Human Kinetics.

TEACHING HINTS

- To make the hunt more challenging and to check for understanding, have students stay connected (by hands or wrists) while performing all the aerobic activities.

- Substitute your school mascot or colors in your hunt activities.

- Add regional or cultural aerobic activities that your students enjoy to your hunt cards.

- Develop aerobic recess challenges for your students to participate in during Heart Month. Share one each day in the announcements or on a bulletin board in the gym or cafeteria.

- Develop a February activity calendar for home or family participation in heart healthy activities.

- Create a "Heart Smart" bulletin board to display heart facts.

- Create bulletin boards to promote Heart Month, such as "Move Around Enough, Eat Healthy Stuff, Live Tobacco Free!" "A Healthy Heart Is a Happy Heart! Don't Sit, Be Fit!!" and "To Be FIT, You Must Think 'FITT'!" Place the displays around the school—library, hallways, office, and so on.

- Contact the American Heart Association to learn more about Healthy Heart Month (www.americanheart.org).

SAMPLE INCLUSION TIP

A child with autism may not like hearing loud music, so place him or her at a group away from the tape or CD player.

ASSESSMENT

- Ask students to complete this statement: Aerobic fitness is the ability of the _____ and _____ to supply _____ to the working muscles over time. (During Healthy Heart Month, the Mind Map can be used so that students continue to learn the definitions.)

- Have students name three aerobic activities that they performed in the hunt.

7.8 Heart Smart Orienteering

INTERMEDIATE LEVEL

February—Aerobic fitness and FITT; benefits of activity; warning signs for heart disease and stroke; cooperative learning.

PURPOSE

Promoting physical activity, developing cognitive knowledge, and participating in health-enhancing physical activity are three goals of the Physical Best program. The Heart Smart Orienteering activity is a fun way to bring closure to Healthy Heart Month and to check to see if students have developed an understanding of aerobic fitness concepts, the FITT principle, and the warning signs for a heart attack and stroke.

RELATIONSHIP TO NATIONAL STANDARDS

Physical Education Standard 4: The student achieves and maintains a health-enhancing level of fitness.

Health Education Standard 3: The student will demonstrate the ability to practice health-enhancing behaviors and reduce health risks.

EQUIPMENT

- Six to eight cones
- Pencils
- Fun, fast-paced continuous music tape and player
- Physical activity equipment for groups who finish early

Reproducibles

- Orienteering Master Sheet (6 total sheets)
- Heart Smart Orienteering Questions
- FITT Homework Assignment

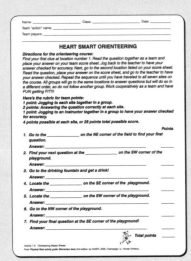

Name three benefits of exercise.

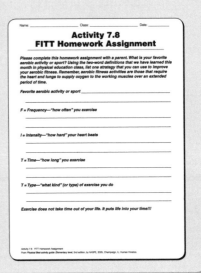

PROCEDURE

1. Students will move from station to station and answer questions related to the key concepts that you have taught in your physical education program.

2. Create an Orienteering Master Sheet based on the number of stations needed and locations to be used. Alternatively, use the samples provided on the CD-ROM by filling in the blanks on each Orienteering Master Sheet with the landmarks specific to your orienteering course and make copies for the students. Each Orienteering Master Sheet will have students moving from station to station, but in a different order.

3. Make sure that students know directions (north, south, east, west) and where to find the key locations (basketball courts, backstop, small slide, drinking fountain, and so on) around your school and playground that you have included on your Orienteering Master Sheets.

4. Place the Heart Smart Orienteering Questions at each location.

5. Students will work in groups of four to six or in squads. Designate a group leader.

6. Each group needs an Orienteering Master Sheet and a pencil.

7. Students begin by jogging together to the first location on their sheet. A Heart Smart Orienteering Question to answer will be at the location. Students agree on an answer, write it on their worksheet, and then return to you to receive their point total before moving on to the next location. The Orienteering Master Sheet lists the rubric for receiving points.

8. Play some fun, fast-paced, continuous music. The activity may take close to 10 minutes to complete, so plan accordingly. Have an aerobic activity planned for students to participate in when their group has completed the activity (individual, partner, or long jump ropes; jump bands; and so on).

© Human Kinetics

TEACHING HINTS

■ Orienteering combines walking, jogging, and map-reading skills. In this activity, we have used directions and playground markers as the checkpoints rather than a compass. If you have used compasses to teach orienteering with your intermediate students, change the sites and checkpoints to make the activity more challenging.

■ Color coding or numbering each of the student Orienteering Worksheets will allow you to create a master answer sheet when students come to you to share their answers and receive their points.

■ This activity lends itself to differentiation. Let students choose their own groups. Students like to work with friends or others who like to jog at the same pace as they do.

■ Always include fun stations (getting a drink, sliding down the slide, and so on) to make the activity more enjoyable for the students.

■ You may need to change the markers (locations) on your orienteering sheets to match playground locations at your school.

SAMPLE INCLUSION TIP

Have a student who is visually impaired use a wand or baton and jog with a different student each time the group travels to a new site.

ASSESSMENT

This activity is itself an assessment. To check to be sure that all students worked together on the activity, ask a few of the Heart Smart Orienteering Questions as students line up to be dismissed for the day:

■ Who can tell me what each of the letters in FITT stands for?

■ What is one warning sign for a heart attack or stroke?

■ Name three aerobic activities.

7.9 Everyday and Sometimes Foods

INTERMEDIATE LEVEL

March—Nutrition and food choices using the food pyramid.

PURPOSE

March is National Nutrition Month and a great month to incorporate body composition and nutrition education concepts in your physical education program. The Everyday and Sometimes Foods Activity will help students understand basic nutritional concepts while participating in healthy, physical activity. The Treat Challenge included in the reproducible is a family extension assignment from this activity that will allow students to set a goal for improving food choices at home using the food pyramid as a guide.

RELATIONSHIP TO NATIONAL STANDARDS

Health Education Standard 3: The student will demonstrate the ability to practice health-enhancing behaviors and reduce health risks.

EQUIPMENT

- Pictures of a variety of foods (can have students bring these to class, in addition to those that you find)
- Four hula hoops for corners and two hula hoops or buckets
- Fast-paced, continuous music and player (The Dole 5 A Day songs would be great reinforcers for this activity, see www.dole5aday.com for more information.)
- Pencils

PROCEDURE

1. Set out a variety of pictures of everyday and sometimes foods in hula hoops at the four corners of the activity area.

Reproducibles

- Everyday and Sometimes Foods Assessment
- Treat Challenge Sheets (family homework)

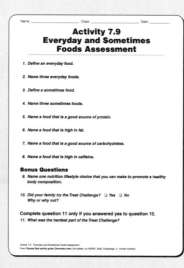

2. Divide the class into four groups. Assign each group a corner of the activity area to work from.

3. In the center of the activity area, place two hula hoops or buckets—one for everyday foods and one for sometimes foods.

4. Use a fun, fast-paced, continuous music tape.

5. On the "Go" signal or when the music begins, all students pick up one food picture item from their corners, jog to the center of the activity area, and drop them in the correct everyday or sometimes hoop or bucket.

6. Students jog back to their corners, get another food item, and repeat the sequence until they move all food items or time is up.

7. This is not a relay. All students are active throughout the game and pick up only one food item at a time.

© Human Kinetics

TEACHING HINTS

■ To make your food pictures, use a clip art program, cut pictures from newspapers and magazines, or ask students to bring in pictures of their favorite foods.

■ Use some of the cultural foods that are prominent in your region of the country.

■ Visit your local Dairy Council to get visual aids that will support the teaching of Physical Best concepts and nutrition education. The Dairy Council has great food graphics that will reinforce the concepts taught in this activity.

■ For a variation, have students practice specific locomotor skills or dance steps as they move to and from their corners while playing the game.

■ To increase the difficulty for older students, have four to five hoops or buckets in the center of the activity area and have students identify the nutritional component found in the food item on each card (carbohydrates, protein, fats, water, and so on).

■ Create a fun bulletin board: "Eat Wise and Exercise!" Have the activity and food pyramids posted for use throughout the month while teaching the Physical Best body composition and nutrition education concepts.

■ Work with your classroom teachers (food services also) to coordinate nutrition concepts taught in the health curriculum with concepts taught in your Physical Best program.

■ Although March is National Nutrition Month, you could use the Treat Challenge during the holidays or as a summer challenge.

SAMPLE INCLUSION TIPS

▨ For a student with visual impairments, use bright signs on the cones and buckets that contrast with the surrounding environment. Have a student who is blind work with a peer and have the peer read the food item on each card. Let the student who is blind determine if the food is an everyday food or a sometimes food.

▨ Offer less intense locomotor movements and shorten the distances traveled to accomodate students who have difficulty traveling (includes asthma and obesity).

ASSESSMENT

▨ Have students complete this statement: Body composition is the _____ (define body composition). To maintain a healthy body composition, you must _____ and _____.

▨ For closure at the end of the activity, have a few students pick out foods from each of the buckets or hoops in the center and check results as a class. Name the foods and have students explain what section of the food pyramid they belong in.

▨ Use the formal assessment included in the CD-ROM reproducible to see if students can define everyday and sometimes foods and give examples of each.

7.10   Spring Into Fitness

INTERMEDIATE LEVEL

April—Total fitness circuit; benefits of activity and risks associated with inactivity.

PURPOSE

Students and adults will make many choices that affect personal health and physical well-being throughout their lifetimes. Some of these choices lead to longer life expectancy; others negatively affect health. In this springtime cooperative learning fitness activity, students will learn about many healthy benefits of activity and risks associated with inactivity and poor lifestyle choices. To add to the fun for your students and bring this spring fitness activity to life, use the Energizer Bunny as your role model for healthy choices.

RELATIONSHIP TO NATIONAL STANDARDS

Physical Education Standard 3: The student participates regularly in physical activity.

Physical Education Standard 6: The student values physical activity for health, enjoyment, challenge, self-expression, and/or social interaction.

EQUIPMENT

- One large bucket or box
- Four hula hoops (red, blue, green, and yellow for corners)
- Jump ropes, variety of types and sizes of balls, resistive exercise bands
- Fun, continuous music with a spring theme and player (One fun song is called "Danger Zone," which seems appropriate because this activity involves an element of risk.)

PROCEDURE

1. Place the bucket in the middle of the activity area and fill it with the task cards. Place the four colored hula hoops in the four corners of the activity area.

2. Explain to the students that they are to work in groups and try to build a healthy body by exercising and making good lifestyle choices.

3. Divide the class into four groups. Each group goes to a separate work corner. You can use squads or let students work with friends for this activity. Designate a team leader.

4. Choose a fun, upbeat song to play.

5. When the music begins, each team leader designates a student to jog to the big bucket to pick up a task card. The student jogs back

Reproducible

- Spring Into Fitness Task Cards

Benefits of Physical Activity—
More Energy

1. Jog once around the activity area as a group. Encourage other students as you pass by them!
2. Use a jump rope and practice your favorite skills for one minute. Can you put five skills together in a mini-routine?
3. Physical fitness is the ability to work and play with _____ to spare!

Activity 7.10 Spring Into Fitness Task Cards
From *Physical Best activity guide: Elementary level*, 2nd edition, by NASPE, 2005, Champaign, IL: Human Kinetics.

to the group and shares with the group the benefit or risk that is on the task card. The benefit or risk will include an activity to perform, a question to answer, or both. The whole group works together to perform the task.

6. The team leader picks a new student to jog to the bucket, and the group repeats the activity. Let each student in the group pick up at least one or two task cards. Set a time limit for the whole fitness activity.

© Human Kinetics

TEACHING HINTS

■ Change the intensity by having two or more students stay connected (by hands or wrists) and jog to the center to get the task cards. Alternatively, use more hula hoops and have six to eight groups. This setup will allow students to be more active and contribute more to group success.

■ Add some fun and novel activities that your students enjoy or have access to on your task cards (rock wall, pull-up bar, unicycles, stationary bikes, and so on).

■ Change the activity to include holidays or physical education activity celebrations (Valentine's Day, PE and Sport Week, and so on).

■ Create a fun bulletin board: "Spring into Fitness!" Use the Energizer Bunny as your visual along with the words "Exercise Keeps Your Heart Going and Going and Going!!!"

SAMPLE INCLUSION TIPS

■ When working with a child with autism, "rethink" the basic skills and tasks listed on your task cards. For instance, when dribbling, allow the student to use a larger ball, use two hands, or let him or her walk forward, drop and catch the ball while other students work on continuous dribbling skills. Students who are autistic can help set up, put equipment away, and have many choices like their peers.

■ To help a student with cerebral palsy, put some of the task cards on a chair in the center so that they do not have to reach so low to get a task card.

ASSESSMENT

■ Ask a few students, "Why do you exercise?" Then ask, "Will class members give different reasons? Why or why not?"

■ Have students name three benefits of exercise.

■ Ask students to name three risks associated with a lack of exercise or poor lifestyle choices.

■ Have students name one lifestyle choice that they can make to improve their personal fitness level.

■ Have students list the top three benefits of exercise they learned about from this activity or have them draw a picture and name the benefit most important to them. Display the samples for students, staff, and the school community to view.

■ As the students line up to leave class, have each student name one healthy benefit of activity and one risk associated with inactivity.

7.11 Project ACES

PRIMARY AND INTERMEDIATE LEVELS

May—Cooperative learning; activity celebration.

PURPOSE

Many AAHPERD and physical activity celebrations in America promote regular physical activity and fitness in our schools and communities. Project ACES was developed by Len Saunders, a New Jersey physical education teacher. His mission was for schools throughout America (and now the world) to drop everything and exercise (All Children Exercising Simultaneously) on the first Wednesday in May each year. You can access the ACES Web site (www.projectaces.com) to get ideas on ways to promote the event and learn about some tried and true sample activities. The Exercise Hunt is a great schoolwide fitness activity that promotes cooperative learning while participating in an activity "for the health of it." Pairing up a primary and intermediate class adds to the fun for students and staff as they celebrate a healthy dose of health-related fitness exercises and activities. You can teach the hunt ahead of time or use it as a novel activity exclusively for your Project ACES activity.

RELATIONSHIP TO NATIONAL STANDARDS

Physical Education Standard 3: The student participates regularly in physical activity.

EQUIPMENT

Fast-paced, continuous music and player

PROCEDURE

1. Plan your Project ACES activity with your principal at least a month in advance. Discuss changes in the daily schedule.

2. Plan and prepare the staff a few weeks ahead of the big day. Send a diagram and note to classroom teachers a week in advance. Pair up intermediate and primary classes and let teachers know where their designated spot will be to participate in the ACES activity.

3. Make the Exercise Hunt Task Cards. Depending on the size of the school, you can use the ones provided on the CD-ROM, or you can make more by cutting and pasting so that no two groups follow the same order. You can also make up a variety of hunt cards with different activities on them. Choose what will work best at your school and with your students and staff.

Reproducible

- Exercise Hunt Task Cards

Stay linked at all times!
- Skip and perform the human clock three times in both directions.
- Do 10 triceps push-ups.
- Perform the sit-and-reach stretch (30 seconds on each leg).
- Tag five people wearing red.
- Jog around the court two times.
- Stand up and sit down five times.
- Do 15 small arm circles forward and backward.
- Touch five different lines on the court.
- Try 10 four-count sit-ups (with knees bent, touch knees, toes, knees, and back).
- Follow the leader. Do the giraffe stretch for 30 seconds (reach tall).
- Say, "I love PE" 10 times.

Have fun getting fit!
7 days without exercise makes one "weak."
Be active for the "health of it!"

Activity 7.11 Exercise Hunt Cards
From *Physical Best activity guide: Elementary level, 2nd edition,* by NASPE, 2005, Champaign, IL: Human Kinetics.

4. Make sure that the students know how to perform new and novel ideas that you have included in the hunt. Demonstrate and practice the activities in physical education class before ACES day. For example, the "human clock" (as directed in an Exercise Hunt Task Card) is a cooperative learning activity where the class makes a circle holding hands or wrists and then runs quickly three times clockwise and three times counterclockwise.

5. Let all classes make their way out to the playground. After all are ready to begin, put on some fun, upbeat music and let the whole school enjoy 10 to 15 minutes of fun physical activity.

TEACHING HINTS

- The designated time to participate in ACES is 10:15 a.m. local time. You can adjust the time, however, depending on your school schedule and local weather.
- Send a reminder notice home the day before your event (good public relations) so that all students dress for physical activity on Project ACES day.
- Use your school colors to make your hunt cards.
- Many schools have reading buddies in which primary and intermediate classes work together all year. Check to see if any of your classes are already doing primary-intermediate peer activities and use those pairings on ACES day.
- Take many pictures and display them after the celebration!

SAMPLE INCLUSION TIP

Share new "novel" ideas ahead of time to allow students to practice and create adaptations as needed. Consider the environment.

ASSESSMENT

Encourage teachers to discuss and reinforce the purpose of the activity with their class at the end of the day.

7.12 Catch the Thrill of the Skill

INTERMEDIATE LEVEL

May—The first week is National Physical Education and Sport Week. HRF and SRF circuit motor-skill themes integration.

PURPOSE

The National Association for Sport and Physical Education (NASPE), a national association of AAHPERD, annually celebrates National Physical Education and Sport Week on May 1 through 7 throughout the United States. Each year a different theme is chosen to promote the benefits of quality physical education and sport programs. Check the NASPE Web site (www.aahperd.org/naspe) to learn more about this celebration and to order the National Physical Education and Sport Week Poster.

National Physical Education and Sport Week is a great week to reinforce Physical Best concepts in your health-related physical education program. Be creative and develop a new and fun fitness activity for students to participant in this week! In this activity, health-related fitness and skill-related fitness components are combined to create a total fitness circuit. Also, a few of the skill themes (dribble, strike, and so on) are integrated into the station activities to reinforce motor-skill development.

RELATIONSHIP TO NATIONAL STANDARDS

Physical Education Standard 4: The student achieves and maintains a health-enhancing level of fitness.

EQUIPMENT

- 45-15 or 45-45 segmented music tape and player
- Balls—soccer ball, basketball, tennis ball, hacky sack, and so on
- Tennis rackets
- Tumbling mats
- Jump ropes
- Stopwatches
- Four or five coins
- Specialty equipment—pedometers, steps

PROCEDURE

1. Create the activities that you will use at each of the health-related fitness and skill-related fitness stations. You can have one activity for all students to participate in or a menu of activities at each station.

2. Make a music tape segmented with rest periods (45 seconds-15 seconds or 45-45).

3. Place the signs and equipment in the activity area.

Reproducible

- Health-Related and Skill-Related Fitness Station Signs

Aerobic Fitness

Motor skill—Dribble with hands or feet.

Use a soccer ball or basketball—Dribble back and forth across the activity area. Control the ball!

Aerobic activities—Power walk with a pedometer, do a step routine, jump rope, or jog.

Activity 7.12 Health-Related and Skill-Related Fitness Station Signs
From Physical Best activity guide: Elementary level, 2nd edition, by NASPE, 2005, Champaign, IL: Human Kinetics

4. Explain the station activities to your students.

5. Divide students into groups. Assign each group to a starting station.

6. When the music begins, students perform the station activities.

7. When the music stops, students clean up and then rotate to the next station.

8. If you use a 45-15 music tape, students move directly to next station and begin new activity.

9. Because the circuit has 12 or 13 stations, this activity may take two days to complete, depending on how much time you devote to fitness development activities in your daily lesson.

TEACHING HINTS

▪ Add a free choice station. Place some of your specialty equipment here, student favorites, or activities played in your region of the country (hockey dribbling, juggling, and so on) and let students enjoy personally meaningful or challenging activities!

▪ Create a menu of activities from simple to complex for each station that integrates motor skills based on skill ability (for example, soccer dribbling, basic dribbling, dribble with inside-inside-outside-outside of the foot pattern, advanced dribbling skills). Allow students who play sports outside school to demonstrate intermediate or advanced skills that could be included in stations as a challenge activity.

▪ With fifth-grade students, develop a worksheet and let students keep track of their individual point totals at the stations. On day 2, encourage students to improve their point totals by increasing the intensity of their workloads.

▪ Integrate a character education message or word of the day to promote fair play as part of the week's learning activities and experiences. Many different programs are used throughout the country to teach fair play, character education, and life skills (respect, responsibility, fairness, perseverance, caring, citizenship, integrity, and so forth).

SAMPLE INCLUSION TIP

Children with Down syndrome will experience more success by staying at one station for two to three rotations to minimize transitions. At dribbling stations, slow the movement of the motor skill being practiced, use fleece balls instead of soccer balls for foot-eye coordination activities, and use a basketball inside a net bag for hand-eye coordination activities.

ASSESSMENT

■ Have students define health-related fitness and skill-related fitness (fifth grade).

■ Have students name three sports that require participants to utilize both health-related fitness and skill-related fitness components. Ask which health-related fitness and skill-related fitness components are necessary.

■ Ask, "Based on your participation in this total fitness circuit, which component of health-related fitness and skill-related fitness do you feel very competent in? Which do you need to improve in?"

■ Have students name three activities or sports that require participants to utilize aerobic fitness.

■ Have students name three activities or sports that require participants to utilize muscular endurance or muscular strength.

■ Have students name three sports or activities that require participants to utilize flexibility.

7.13   Dash for Cash

PRIMARY/INTERMEDIATE

May or June—End of the year celebration. HR Fitness components; activity celebration.

PURPOSE

The Physical Best program provides teachers and students with a variety of enjoyable fitness development activities while meeting school, school district, and state and national standards for physical education. After a full year of learning Physical Best education concepts, participating in health-related fitness assessment activities, and setting personal goals to maintain or improve fitness levels and healthy habits, students need a fun physical activity to celebrate their year of "moving to learn" and "learning to move." Dash for Cash integrates health-related fitness components and math skills in an action-packed activity. All students are active and make healthy and personally meaningful fitness choices while learning about the value of money and honesty.

RELATIONSHIP TO NATIONAL STANDARDS

Physical Education Standard 3: The student participates regularly in physical activity.

Physical Education Standard 4: The student achieves and maintains a health-enhancing level of fitness.

EQUIPMENT

- One box for the bank
- Copy and laminate 100 $1 bills. You can NOT legally copy real $1 bills, so use play money to make your copies or buy some play money from a store.
- Three tumbling mats
- Six jump ropes
- Aerobic steps (or folded mats)
- Beanbags
- Fun, fast-paced music focusing on summer fun and player (Any song by the Beach Boys works well.)
- Activity equipment for free-choice stations

PROCEDURE

1. Place the Dash for Cash Fitness Station Signs and equipment around the activity area.

2. Students line up around the perimeter of the activity area on the boundary lines if available.

Reproducible

- Dash for Cash Fitness Station Signs

Aerobic Fitness

Stay active for two minutes. Watch the clock!

- **Develop a short jump rope routine. Try to put together 5 to 10 of the jump rope skills that you have learned this year in physical education class.**

- **Use the aerobic steps or a folded mat and keep moving for two minutes. Add your arms to increase the intensity of your workout.**

Activity 7.13 Dash for Cash Fitness Station Signs
From Physical Best activity guide: Elementary level, 2nd edition, by NASPE, 2005, Champaign, IL: Human Kinetics.

---

3. The banker (teacher) stands at one end of the activity area with money in the banker's box.

4. Students walk, jog, or run around the perimeter of the activity area at a pace that is good for them. Each time students complete one lap, they receive $1 from the banker.

5. After students complete three laps, they can choose whether to keep moving or pay the banker and go to one of the health-related fitness stations to exercise.

6. The object of the activity is for students to have participated in all the health-related fitness stations before the allotted time is up. Each station costs $3 to participate in (much like adults pay a monthly fee to join a fitness club).

7. Students pay the banker each time they go to a new fitness station. Students can choose different strategies for participation. They can move aerobically and receive lots of money before spending it to participate in the fitness stations, or they can move, exercise, move, exercise, until they are finished.

8. If time remains after some students are done with the fitness stations, add a few free choice stations that might cost more money ($5) and let students choose a favorite motor skill or piece of equipment to work with (rock wall, juggling scarves, tennis skills, two square and so on).

TEACHING HINTS

▓ With slight modifications, this activity can be used with all elementary grades. Primary students need more time to complete the activity. They also need a different menu of exercises and activities to participate in based on their ability levels. You should be the banker with younger students to make sure that all students receive and spend the correct amount of money. When students are ready to participate in a fitness station, they will count the money back to you.

▓ Pairing up intermediate and primary classes is another way that younger students can participate in the activity. You would need to work out the schedule for this activity ahead of time with classroom teachers.

▓ This activity teaches the life skill of honesty. After intermediate students have participated in the activity with your help, try it without a banker at the box. Building trust with students is a benefit to this modification. You can also monitor the fitness stations better.

▓ Make some copies of larger bills ($5 and $10) and give those out to students as you see fit (developing a steady pace while moving, helping another student, working with a student with special needs, putting equipment away properly, and so forth).

■ Talk about intensity with your students on day 2. Challenge students to work a little harder and make more money so that they have time to participate in one of the free choice stations.

■ If you teach using skill themes, create motor-skill stations (catch, throw, strike, dribble, and so on) as part of your free choice stations.

■ Dash for Cash would be a great activity for a family fitness night to promote National Physical Fitness and Sports Month. Create some free choice sport stations for families to participate in.

■ You also can use Dash for Cash at the end of the year to promote lifelong and leisure (recreational) activities that students may want to participate in during the upcoming summer months. With this variation, each activity has a different dollar value depending on the intensity of the activity (bowling $3, rock wall $5, beach ball volleyball $6, tennis striking skills $7, and so on). Post signs at each station with the name of the activity, directions, and cost to play. You may also want to post a menu of activities at the bank so that students can read the activities and their cost each time they complete a lap.

SAMPLE INCLUSION TIPS

■ A student in a wheelchair could receive $2 per lap rather than $1 because it takes them longer to complete the task.

■ Working with a peer helper will help keep students with a disability safe and more comfortable as they move around the perimeter of the activity area.

ASSESSMENT

■ Have students name one aerobic, flexibility, and muscular strength and muscular endurance activity that they performed.

■ Ask students how they increased their intensity at one of the fitness stations.

7.14

Summer Fun— Summer Shape-Up Challenge

PRIMARY AND INTERMEDIATE LEVELS

June, July, or August—Benefits of activity and risks of inactivity.

PURPOSE

Physical fitness is a journey, not a destination! The school year has ended, but we want students to develop active, healthy lifestyles year round. The Summer Fun—Summer Shape-Up Challenge integrates classroom subject matter and gives students and their families a variety of ideas for participating in health-enhancing physical activity during the summer months. Remember: Seven days without exercise makes one "weak!"

RELATIONSHIP TO NATIONAL STANDARDS

Physical Education Standard 3: The student participates regularly in physical activity.

Health Education Standard 3: The student will demonstrate the ability to practice health-enhancing behaviors and reduce health risks.

PROCEDURE

1. Use school letterhead or fun summer paper to create your Summer Shape-Up Challenge.

2. Hand out the activity to each class during the last week of school. Challenge students to try the activity for two months. Invite students to return their completed challenge sheets when the new school year begins.

TEACHING HINTS

■ You can create a calendar to change the format of the challenge.

■ You can develop a completely new set of activities for month 2.

■ Incorporate academic strategies (reading, writing, math) that your school has focused on during the year into your challenge activity.

■ Incorporate personal responsibility, life skills, or character education traits that your school has focused on during the year into your challenge activity (National Standards for Physical Education 5 and 6).

Reproducible

■ Summer Shape-Up Challenge Activity Sheet

Activity 7.14
Healthy Bodies, Healthy Minds
Summer Shape-Up Challenge

As the school year ends, we hope that all our students and their families will enjoy a relaxing and fun summer break. Stay active by trying these Healthy Body, Healthy Minds Summer Shape-Up Challenges. In the first month of break place a check mark by each activity you complete. In the second month of break place a star by each activity you complete. Set a goal to be active at least five or six days per week!
—*Physical Education Teacher*

Exercise Your Options This Summer—CHOOSE to Be FIT!

1. Jog one lap around the block (drink water before, during, and after you exercise).
2. Play a **two** versus one game.
3. Make **three** baskets in a row.
4. Run **four** sets of stairs.
5. "**Five** a day keeps the doctor away." Eat five fruits and vegetables today!
6. Throw and hit a target **six** times.
7. Perform **seven** different stretches (hold each stretch for 10 to 30 seconds).
8. Play a game of catch with a friend! Can you catch **eight** in a row?
9. The word that sounds like "**nine**" in German means "no." How many laps can you jog around the inside of your house with no stops?
10. Hold a push-up position for **10** seconds from three different positions!
11. Eat 6 to **11** servings from the bread and grain group today!
12. Jump a rope **12** times your age. Is your heart beating fast or slow?
13. Perform your favorite exercise for **13** seconds or 13 times!
14. Try to complete **14** curl-ups in 30 seconds.
15. Read a book for **15** minutes!
16. Perform **16** wall push-ups. Have someone (about the same size as you) lean against your back to challenge you to work a little harder!
17. Practice **17** cartwheels, alternating from the left and right sides.
18. Think about **18** spelling words you learned this year in school. Try some push-up fun with a friend or family member and spell each word!
19. Commercialize today. During a one-hour TV show, do **19** jumping jacks during each commercial break!
20. Practice your math facts with a family member or friend for **20** minutes!
21. Perform **21** vertical power jumps. Bend your knees and use your arms. How high can you jump?
22. Perform **22** zigzag jumps in four different directions.
23. Hold the wall sit for **23** seconds. Repeat the exercise three times!
24. Practice bouncing a ball **24** times. How many fancy ways can you bounce it?
25. Spend **25** minutes today writing stories or poems!
26. Strike a ball with a paddle **26** times. Can you do it keeping one foot in place?
27. Go for a **27**-minute walk with your family!
28. How many seconds does it take to throw and catch a ball off a wall **28** times? Repeat the activity three times. Can you improve your time?
29. Measure off **29** feet. How many standing long jumps with your feet together does it take to cover 29 feet?
30. Raise your heart rate **30** beats and try to keep it there for 10 minutes!
31. Write down **31** activities that you can do to improve your health!

Seven days without exercise makes one weak!

Activity 7.14 Summer Shape-Up Challenge Activity Sheet
From *Physical Best activity guide (Elementary level, 3rd edition, by NASPE, 2005, Champaign, IL: Human Kinetics*

SAMPLE INCLUSION TIP

Send a letter to parents offering modifications for students with special needs. Give examples of activities that these children have accomplished in physical education class during the year.

ASSESSMENT

- At the start of the new school year, discuss the summer challenge with returning students. Ask for feedback on participation and physical activities in which the students participated during the summer.
- Collect completed activity sheets and discuss observations about activities and their connection to classroom subject matter.

© Human Kinetics

ADDITIONAL RESOURCES ON CD-ROM

Physical Best's A-B-Cs of Fitness

It's As Easy As A-B-C!

A is for ... Aerobic Fitness
B is for ... Body Composition
C is for ... Cool-Down
D is for ... Developmental Influences
E is for ... Exercises You Enjoy!
F is for ... Flexibility, Frequency
G is for ... Goal Setting
H is for ... Health-Related Fitness
I is for ... Intensity
J is for ... Journey
K is for ... Knowledge
L is for ... Lifestyle Management
M is for ... Metabolism, Muscular Endurance, Muscular Strength
N is for ... Nutrition
O is for ... Overload
P is for ... Physical Activity, Progression
Q is for ... Quest to Be Your Physical Best!
R is for ... Repetitions and Resistance
S is for ... Skill-Related Fitness
T is for ... Time, Type
U is for ... Understanding
V is for ... Value
W is for ... Warm-Up
X is for ... "X"tra Effort
Y is for ... Year Round
Z is for ... Zest to Be Your Physical Best!

ABCs of Fitness
From *Physical Best activity guide: Elementary level*, 2nd edition, by NASPE, 2005, Champaign, IL: Human Kinetics.

ABCs of Fitness

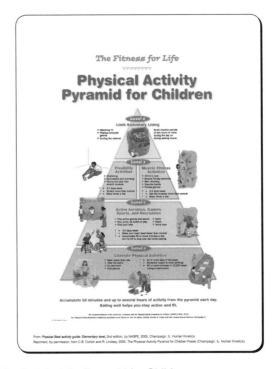

From *Physical Best activity guide: Elementary level*, 2nd edition, by NASPE, 2005, Champaign, IL: Human Kinetics.
Reprinted, by permission, from C.B. Corbin and R. Lindsey, 2005, The Physical Activity Pyramid for Children Poster (Champaign, IL: Human Kinetics).

Physical Activity Pyramid for Children

Reprinted, by permission, from C. Corbin and R. Lindsey, 2004, *Fitness for Life*, 5th ed. (Champaign, IL: Human Kinetics).

REFERENCES

Alter, M.J. 1998. *Sport stretch*. 2nd ed. Champaign, IL: Human Kinetics.

American Academy of Pediatrics (AAP) Committee on Sports Medicine and Fitness. 2001. "Policy Statement: Strength Training by Children and Adolescents." *Pediatrics* 107 (6): 1470-1472.

American College of Sports Medicine (ACSM). 2000. *ACSM's Guidelines for exercise testing and prescription*. 6th edition. Baltimore: Lippincott, Williams and Wilkins.

Bailey, R.C., J. Olson, S.L. Pepper, J. Porszaz, T.J. Barstow, and D.M. Cooper. 1995. The Level and Tempo of Children's Physical Activities: An Observational Study. *Medicine and science in sport and exercise* 27: 1033-1041.

Bar-Or, O. 1993. "Importance of Differences Between Children and Adults for Exercise Testing and Exercise Prescription." pp. 57-74 in *Exercise testing and exercise prescription for special cases*, 2nd edition, ed. J.S. Skinner. Philadelphia, PA: Lea and Febiger.

Bar-Or, O. 1994. "Childhood and Adolescent Physical Activity and Fitness and Adult Risk Profile." pp. 931-942 in *International proceedings and consensus statement*, ed. C. Bouchard, R.J. Shephard, and T. Stephens. Champaign, IL: Human Kinetics.

Bar-Or, O., and R.M. Malina. 1995. "Activity, Health and Fitness of Children and Adolescents." pp. 79-123 in *Child health, nutrition, and physical activity*, ed. L. W.Y. Cheung, J.B. Richmond. Champaign, IL: Human Kinetics.

Blair, S.N., H.W. Kohl, 3rd, C.E. Barlow, R.S. Paffenbarger, Jr., L.W. Gibbons, and C.A. Macera. 1995. "Changes in Physical Fitness and All-Cause Mortality: A Prospective Study of Healthy and Unhealthy Men." *JAMA* 273: 1093-98.

Blanchard, Y. 1999. Health-Related Fitness for Children and Adults with Cerebral Palsy. *American College of Sports Medicine current comment*, August.

Bompa, T.O. 2000. *Total training for young champions*. Champaign, IL: Human Kinetics.

Boreham, C.A., J. Twisk, M. Savage, G.W. Cran, and J.J. Strain. 1997. "Physical Activity, Sports Participation, and Risk Factors in Adolescents." *Medicine and science in sport and exercise* 29: 788-793.

Boreham, C.A., J. Twisk, L. Murray, M. Savage, J.J. Strain, and G.W. Cran. 2001. "Fitness, Fatness, and Coronary Heart Disease Risk in Adolescents: The Northern Ireland Young Hearts Project." *Medicine and science in sport and exercise* 33: 270-274.

California Department of Education. 2002. www.cde.ca.gov/news/releases2002/rel37.asp

The Cooper Institute. 2004. *FITNESSGRAM/ACTIVITYGRAM test administration manual*. 3rd ed., ed. Gregory J. Welk and Marilu D. Meredith. Champaign, IL: Human Kinetics.

Corbin, C.B., and R.P. Pangraxi. 2002. Physical Activity for Children: How Much is Enough? In *FITNESSGRAM reference guide*, ed. G.J. Welk, R.J. Morrow, and H.B. Falls, 7. Dallas: The Cooper Institute.

Faigenbaum, A.D., W.J. Kraemer, B. Cahill, J. Chandler, J. Dziados, L.D. Elfink, E. Forman, et al. 1996. Youth resistance training: Position statement paper and literature review. *Strength and conditioning* 18(6): 62-75.

Gardner, H. 1993. *Multiple intelligences: The theory in practice*. New York: Basic Books.

Hass, C.J., M.S. Faigenbaum, and B.A. Franklin. 2001. Prescription of Resistance Training for Healthy Populations. *Sports medicine* 31(14): 953-964.

Heyward, V.H. 2002. *Advanced fitness assessment an exercise prescription*. 4th ed. Champaign, IL: Human Kinetics.

Joint Committee on National Health Education Standards. 1995. *National health education standards: Achieving health literacy*. Atlanta, GA: American Cancer Society.

Knudson, D.V., P. Magnusson, and M. McHugh. 2000. "Current Issues in Flexibility Fitness." pp. 1-8 in *The President's council on physical fitness and sports digest*, series 3, no. 10, ed. C. Corbin and B. Pangrazi. Washington, DC: Department of Health and Human Services.

Kraemer, W. J., and S.J. Fleck. 1993. *Strength training for young adults*. Champaign, IL: Human Kinetics.

National Association for Sport and Physical Education (NASPE). 2004b. *Moving into the future: National standards for physical education,* 2nd ed. Reston, VA: Author.

National Association for Sport and Physical Education (NASPE). 1992. *Outcomes of quality physical education programs.* Reston, VA: Author.

National Association for Sport and Physical Education (NASPE). 2004a. *Physical activity for children: A statement of guidelines for children ages 5-12,* 2nd ed. Reston, VA: Author.

National Association for Sport and Physical Education (NASPE) 2005. *Physical education for lifelong fitness: The Physical Best teachers guide.* Champaign, IL: Human Kinetics.

National Dance Association. *National standards for dance education: What every young american should know and be able to do in dance* (1996). Reston, VA: Author.

National Strength and Conditioning Association. 1985. "Position Statement on Prepubescent Strength Training." *National strength and conditioning association journal* 7: 27-31.

Rowland, T.W. 1996. *Developmental exercise physiology.* Champaign, IL: Human Kinetics.

Sothern, M.S., M. Loftin, R.M. Suskind, J.N. Udall, and U. Becker. 1999. "The Health Benefits of Physical Activity in Children and Adolescents: Implications for Chronic Disease Prevention." *European journal of pediatrics* 158: 271-274.

U.S. Department of Health and Human Services (USDHHS). 1996. "Physical Activity and Health: A Report of the Surgeon General." U.S. Department of Health and Human Services, Centers for Disease Control and Prevention, National Center for Chronic Disease Prevention and Health Promotion. Atlanta: U.S. Department of Health and Human Services, Government Printing Office.

Weiss, M. "Motivating Kids in Physical Activity," *Research digest* (President's Council on Physical Fitness and Sports), 3; 11(2000), www. fitness.gov/digest900.pdf.

Wilson, G., McKay, H., Waddell, L., Notte, J., and Petit, M. 2000. The Health Benefits of a "Healthy Bones" Physical Education Curriculum. In *Physical and health education,* Autumn.

Winnick, J.P., and F.X. Short, eds. 1999. *The Brockport physical fitness training guide.* Champaign, IL: Human Kinetics.

Zwiren, L.D. 1988. "Exercise Prescription for Children". pp. 309-14 in *Resource Manual for guidelines for exercise testing and prescription,* ed. American College of Sports Medicine. Philadelphia: Lea

ABOUT PHYSICAL BEST

Physical Best is a comprehensive health-related fitness education program developed by physical educators for physical educators. Physical Best was designed to educate, challenge, and encourage all children in the knowledge, skills, and attitudes needed for a healthy and fit life. The goal of the program is to help students move from dependence to independence and responsibility for their own health and fitness by promoting regular, enjoyable physical activity. The purpose of Physical Best is to educate ALL children regardless of athletic talent, physical and mental abilities, or disabilities. This is implemented through quality resources and professional development workshops for physical educators.

Physical Best is a program of the National Association for Sport and Physical Education (NASPE). A nonprofit membership organization of over 18,000 professionals in the sport and physical education fields, NASPE is an association of the American Alliance for Health, Physical Education, Recreation and Dance dedicated to strengthening basic knowledge about healthy lifestyles among professionals and the general public. Putting that knowledge into action in schools and communities across the nation is critical to improved academic performance, social reform, and the health of individuals.

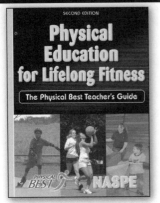
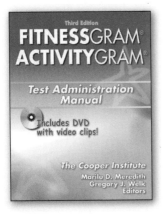